W9-AEZ-585

23.70

95

4-28-95

#28184114

FIELD GUIDE TO MARKETING

Field Guide to Business Terms: *A Glossary of Essential Tools and Concepts for Today's Manager*

Field Guide to Marketing Terms: *A Glossary of Essential Tools and Concepts for Today's Manager*

FIELD GUIDE TO MARKETING:

*A Glossary of Essential Tools
and Concepts
for Today's Manager*

CHIEF CONTRIBUTOR
Tim Hindle

EDITED BY
Alistair D. Williamson

Boston, Massachusetts

Published in the United States by Harvard Business School Press
Copyright © 1994 by The Economist Books Ltd.

Printed in the United States of America

98 97 96 95 94   5 4 3 2 1 (pbk)

98 97 96 95 94   5 4 3 2 1 (hard)

Field Guide to Marketing is part of the Harvard Business/The
Economist Reference Book Series and is based on material first
published in Great Britain in 1993 by The Economist Books Ltd.

The paper used in this publication meets the requirements of the
American National Standard for Permanence of Paper for Printed
Library Materials Z39.49-1984.

Library of Congress Cataloging-in-Publication Data

Hindle, Tim.
    Field guide to marketing : a glossary of essential tools and
concepts for today's manager / chief contributor, Tim Hindle ;
edited by Alistair D. Williamson.
        p. cm. — (Harvard Business/The Economist reference series)
    ISBN 0-87584-435-9 — ISBN 0-87584-430-8 (pbk.)
    1. Marketing—Dictionaries. 2. Marketing—Management—
Dictionaries. I. Williamson, Alistair D. II. Title. III. Series:
Harvard Business/The Economist reference series.
HF5415.H5257   1994
658.8'003—dc20
                                                    93-23865
                                                    CIP

Series design by Mike Fender

CONTENTS

Introduction   *ix*

Part 1   **Marketing in the 1990s**
             The Value of Brands   3
             Advertising   6
             Saving the Swiss Watch   10
Part 2   **Glossary**   17

FIELD GUIDE TO MARKETING

INTRODUCTION

Field Guide to Marketing is the second in a new series of books that bring clarity to the often confusing subject of management.

It is written by Tim Hindle, a former management editor of *The Economist,* and is divided into two parts. The first section is a brief essay that looks at some of the issues most likely to be at the top of marketing managers' agendas in the 1990s. The second section — by far the bulk of the book — is a glossary of the main terms that managers use in their everyday working lives but sometimes feel they do not fully understand.

The book is sprinkled with quotations from both managers and pundits, showing that management is a broad human endeavor with plenty of room for wit and creativity as well as for triumph and disappointment.

In the glossary, words in small capitals usually indicate a separate entry, thus enabling readers to find other relevant information (though they should note that abbreviations and acronyms are also in capitals).

The Harvard Business School Press acknowledges the assistance and contributions of Kenneth L. Bernhardt, Regents' Professor and Chair of the Department of Marketing, Georgia State University, and of Michael Thomas, Professor of Marketing, Strathclyde Business School.

PART 1

MARKETING IN THE 1990s

MARKETING IN THE 1990s

THE VALUE OF BRANDS

There was a peculiar cult in the 1980s that, for want of a better name, could be called "brand worship." Its core belief was that brand names had a great and immutable value that most people had failed to appreciate. It found some of its keenest followers in Europe, which was stuffed with fine old-name products suffering a similar fate as its fine old-name aristocrats.

HIDDEN ASSETS

When the Swiss food-products company Nestlé bought the British confectionery group Rowntree in 1988, it paid well over $1 billion for something that had never appeared on Rowntree's balance sheet: the value of some of the names in its portfolio of products — names like Polo, Kit-Kat, and After Eight.

As this hidden value became more widely recognized, a number of companies decided to put the value of their brands on their balance sheet. The drinks and hotels group Grand Metropolitan added $800 million for a few of its more recently acquired products, such as Smirnoff vodka. When Polly Peck bought the Del Monte fresh-fruit business it added $400 million to its assets for the value of the Del Monte name alone. (Polly Peck subsequently collapsed, in part because it overstretched itself with the Del Monte purchase.)

This practice was not just cosmetic. It improved the companies' leverage and, as a consequence, their ability to borrow from banks and thence their capacity to buy yet more brands.

REPUTATION IS ALL

However, events conspired to bring the brand worshippers down to earth. The value of brands was seen to be far less tangible than the accountants who were using it to puff up balance sheets might have wished. For a start, names can go off faster than a raw steak in Riyadh: sales of Perrier water were decimated in 1990 by the discovery of small quantities of benzene in samples taken from the water's source.

Similarly, the great name of Salomon Brothers was humbled overnight by the 1991 discovery of dirty dealing in its U.S. government securities department. Salomon had few assets but its name and a bunch of screens. Full-page newspaper advertisements with a Japanese-style confession from its new chairman, Warren Buffett, only went part way toward restoring the value of the Salomon brand of securities business.

PRIVATE-BRAND GROWTH

It was not just the vulnerability of brands to unexpected events that reduced their glamour. Market-related events were also working against them. In consumer goods, retailers were gaining the upper hand in their eternal power struggle with manufacturers. In the United Kingdom, in particular, food retailing was becoming increasingly concentrated, with over half of all sales going through a few chains like Sainsbury and Tesco.

These powerful chains found that one way of increasing their profit margins was to have "private-label" products specially manufactured for them. Consumers came to value Safeway's name on a bottle of wine, or Marks & Spencer's St. Michael label on a bar of chocolate quite as highly as the names of any of the well-established manufacturers of these products.

In a time of recession consumers were even more attracted to private-label products by their price, which was always lower than that of the famous-name manufacturers. For the balance-sheet value of these manufacturers' brands essentially lay in the premium that they could charge for attaching their names to the products. That premium could be as high as 50%, and it was always bound to attract potshots.

GLOBAL DREAMS

Another setback for the brand worshippers came from the unexpected difficulties they found in taking brands across borders. In the excitement of globalization, companies anticipated making huge economies of scale from marketing the same brand in the same way around the globe. Any product with a strong market share in one country was fair game for globalization. If products as American as McDonald's and Coca-Cola could do it, then anybody could.

They could not, of course, because not all names travel well. For example, Irish Mist liqueur has a hard time in German-speaking markets ("mist" in German means "manure"). More-over, within the global village that marketing people were blindly assuming already existed, distinct tastes proved remark-ably persistent.

Unilever, which had traditionally rejoiced in allowing its national detergent companies great autonomy to develop their own products, came under the influence of the globalizers and reversed its policy for the launch of Radion, a detergent that was sold on its ability to remove odors as well as dirt. With Radion the company imposed a universally uniform package design and a bright orange color on national managers who were reluctant in many cases.

Since then Unilever has reached a happy compromise with

its international brands. It defines what it sees as a product's "core brand values," those which meet common needs in all its main markets, and then it tinkers with other aspects of the brand according to the needs of different local markets.

THE NEED TO NURTURE

The main lesson of the cult of the brand and its downfall is that brands cannot be left unattended for long. Building them up is a long, hard process and so is maintaining them — a fact that has been ignored by those who have bought an already established brand in the belief that with such-and-such a name they cannot go wrong.

Look at the products on the supermarket shelves that have not had their market shares drastically eroded by private-label products. They include instant coffee and breakfast cereals. The likes of Nescafé and Kellogg have retained their market leadership because they have spent much of the premium in their prices on constantly developing new products and improving existing ones. Then they have spent even more on advertising the fact. The brand that is merely sat upon will soon be squashed.

ADVERTISING

The advertising industry, as much as its own inventions, lives off the impression it creates. Part of that impression used to be that advertising was a worthy profession based on much research into consumer behavior and even more understanding of it. Anybody who knows that women in New York use nearly 30 times as much makeup as women in Vermont must surely know more about consumers than consumers know about themselves.

But the impression that the advertising industry often gave during the 1980s was different: it was the impression of an industry obsessed with growth at almost any price, willing to follow any fad for a quick profit.

KEEPING UP IS HARD TO DO

Admittedly the industry has had to cope with unprecedented pressures. That has made it an enthusiastic follower of the fashion to "go global." When multinational clients such as Unilever and Gillette demanded that the same advertising agency serve them in all their markets, the agencies by and large obliged. Wherever Unilever has gone (which is just about everywhere) so has its main agency, J. Walter Thompson. In Europe alone, JWT has offices in 15 countries. Such an overhead focuses the mind of even the most gentlemanly JWT director firmly on profit.

AFTER THE MASS MARKET . . .

In addition to globalization, the agencies have been trying to come to grips with the death of the "mass market," a sort of essential yeast extract on which they all grew up. Early advertisements were designed to sell Singer sewing machines, Model T Fords, or whatever, in one way to everybody. The economies of scale that enabled companies like Singer and Ford to produce for a mass market also worked in favor of their agencies. The high cost of creating their advertisements could be spread by using the same advertisements widely.

. . . THE ATTRACTIONS OF GLOBALIZATION . . .

The principle carried into globalization; indeed one of its main attractions for manufacturers and their agencies was the further economies of scale it promised. If one advertisement could sell the same product to a housewife in Maine and to a black kid in Louisiana, then it could also sell the product to mothers in Paris, kids in Prague, and housewives in Hong Kong. When Birds Eye made its fish-finger advertisements, it took its famous Cap'n and his crew to the Caribbean and filmed footage for all the world's fish-finger markets. Separate voice-overs coped with different languages, and a single image everywhere helped to reinforce the brand.

. . . THEN ON TO SEGMENTATION

Unfortunately for the agencies, just as they were going global their idea of the mass market had to be revised; industry had discovered "segmentation," the phenomenon of a post-mass-market era in which sophisticated production methods enabled the same product to be "tweaked" almost without limit. That way it could be made to appeal to a large number of small market segments. A fairly uniform commodity-type product like Tylenol, a U.S. over-the-counter drug for headaches, was suddenly extended to include 40 different varieties of the drug, each targeted at a slightly different consumer.

Even the Ford Escort car, rolling off production lines that had invented the mass market, became available in a wide range of models: souped-up models for aggressive make-believe rally drivers; stylish cabriolets for those whose hair looked good in a high wind; and solid reliable models for drivers whose main feat was a weekly trip to the post office.

This segmenting of markets was accompanied by another change that had a strong influence on the advertising industry: the shortening of products' life cycles. For a while nothing was meant to last; all goods were fashion goods, designed to be thrown away as the seasons changed. Swatch turned the watch into a fashion item; and a *Wall Street Journal* headline declared, "IBM to start announcing its fall line."

OPEN SKIES

At the same time the means by which advertisers told the world about their products were changing. A new enthusiasm for deregulating the airwaves brought a host of new television and radio channels, especially in Europe where the state's monopoly of broadcasting had been traditionally tight. Satellites floating over Europe could be broadcasting up to 70 new European television channels by the year 2000.

The new channels fought fiercely for advertising's dollars,

and they were fighting not only with one another but also with commercial radio. Setting up a radio station requires very little capital, and in some countries it seems as if there are already as many channels as there are listeners.

HITTING THE TARGET

Advertisers trying to reach segmented markets favored media with narrow identifiable audiences — black teenagers, women age 35–45, and so on — and the media obliged. "Narrowcasting" grew at the expense of broadcasting. Television provided sports channels, pop-music channels, and prewar movie channels. Radio could cast even more narrowly, reaching (should any advertiser want to) a few hundred jazz fans, or even the 33 people who had never liked anything since their last Perry Como concert.

In this "narrow" world, Levi's could appear in *Vogue* as a high-fashion item for the richest people on earth and at the same time on city-center billboards as a garment for the urban underclass.

MEDIA BARONY

While television and radio were being deregulated into more and more providers of services, the printed media were becoming more concentrated into ever bigger groups. The likes of Murdoch, Maxwell, Hachette, and Bertelsmann created vast new media empires that were no respecters of any division between print and film.

These empires threatened the delicate balance of power between advertisers and the media: as they used their muscle to push up their advertising rates, the agencies responded by pooling their "media-buying" divisions to gain economies of scale and to have more clout in bargaining with the media barons.

The more that economic growth slowed, the more intense became the increasing competition among them for limited advertising budgets. Newspaper barons ran their own advertising campaigns to tell the world how many television viewers were actually asleep, smooching on the couch, or making coffee at a time when they were alleged to be intently watching an advertisement. With so much change taking place, it is perhaps not surprising that some agencies lost their way.

SAVING THE SWISS WATCH

One of the most remarkable marketing stories of recent years is that of the Swatch. The public's perception of the Swatch (a clever elision of Swiss and watch) is that almost single-handedly it saved the venerable Swiss watch industry from extinction, or at least from a quiet retirement on the high-priced shelves of expensive jewelers. And that is not far from the truth.

Immediately after World War II, four out of five watches worn on wrists around the world were made in Switzerland. Switzerland was to the watch what Japan is to the camera. This huge market share had been built up over three centuries of Swiss watchmaking expertise.

Nevertheless it took little more than three decades to knock it down. By the early 1980s, Switzerland was manufacturing only one out of every five watches worn around the world. In 1950, nearly every watch imported into the United States was Swiss. By the mid-1980s, less than 5% of them were Swiss. Almost inevitably, in 1983, the two major Swiss watch companies, Asuag and SSIH, had to be ignominiously rescued by the Swiss banks. They were merged into one company, SMH.

THE ELECTRONIC AGE

Two things had conspired against the Swiss and brought about this dramatic reversal of fortune: technology and price. Although the Swiss invented the electronic watch (the so-called quartz watch) in the late 1960s, it was first manufactured and sold in the United States. As with so many other new products (or quantum leaps in product development), the country of its invention was slower than others to appreciate its market potential.

The first companies to sell electronic watches were American (Hamilton and Timex). But in the 1970s production shifted to Hong Kong and Japan as these Eastern stars were able to undercut their Western rivals and produce highly competitive, low-priced quartz watches. As with so many other electronic products, Western companies were unprepared for the rate at which the price of the quartz technology fell. The Japanese took a substantial market share by reaping vast economies of scale from mass-production and the concentration of the industry in two firms, Citizen and Seiko. Hong Kong rapidly became a bigger production center than Switzerland, thanks to its low labor costs and its willingness to live with wafer-thin margins.

THE SWISS FIGHT BACK

To its credit, the Swiss watch industry did not throw up its hands in despair and retire to live off chocolate and other nations' bank deposits. Even in its darkest hour, as Asuag and SSIH were being rescued, a counterattack was well under way. This came from an old watchmaking company called ETA, a subsidiary of SMH.

In the early 1980s, ETA had decided to launch an innovative new product that would build on the Swiss industry's strengths while taking on board some of the lessons from Japan and Hong Kong's successes. Switzerland's strength lay in its technology. The early quartz watches had been "digital," displaying the time as a series of numbers in a frame. The analog technology required to produce a quartz watch with hands that moved around a face was more complicated, but ETA was a recognized master at it. Market research showed that consumers preferred the continuity of a watch face to the jerky shifts of digital numbers.

The enforced concentration of their watchmaking industry within SMH enabled the Swiss to think, as the Japanese had, of creating a low-priced product that relied on volume sales and aggressive marketing. This was quite revolutionary. Swiss watches had always been discreet and upmarket, with names like Audemars Piguet and Piaget quietly appearing on the back covers of glossy magazines. What did the Swiss know about creating a splash for a flashy cheap watch?

Moreover, many in the industry thought the world watch market was saturated. Although people had long abandoned the idea (on which the quality Swiss watchmakers had once thrived) that they should have only one watch for life, by the early 1980s every American had, on average, three watches. Was this not close to the limit? With millions of unwanted cheap watches pouring out of the Far East, who was going to risk investing in yet more capacity?

THE WATCH AS FASHION

ETA did. It spent heavily on a highly computerized production line to turn out an analog quartz watch with a target ex-factory price of SwFr15. To achieve this, it was necessary to weld the watch into its case. The product was literally unrepairable, the world's first disposable watch. But while the basic watch was to remain the same, an ever-changing range of designs on its face and strap would turn it into fashion-wear.

This was the company's stroke of genius. Its product was going to be different. But it was not going to be differentiated as a timepiece; it was going to be differentiated as the first fashion accessory that happened to tell the time. It was to be like a handbag or a belt, and it was to be replaced according to the fashion and the season.

At the end of 1982, the Swatch was test marketed in a number of U.S. department stores. There was no advertising, and it was met with wide indifference. As a result, several modifications were made. The choice of models and prices was reduced, so much so that by 1986 the Swatch had a single price all over the world. The designs were made much more colorful, with strong sporting associations that directed the Swatch's appeal firmly at the teenage market.

GLOBAL PRODUCT

Then the company began a massive promotion and advertising campaign. It had built into its costing a large margin to pay for the worldwide marketing that it knew its novel product was going to need. In 1985 it spent more than SwFr30m on advertising in the United States alone. Its advertisements were colorful, young, and fresh — and the same ones were adapted for use all over the world. That way the Swatch could develop a universal brand image.

ETA sponsored a number of "style leaders" such as Ivan Lendl at the U.S. Open tennis championship and other characters at less-conventional events — for example, subaquatic ballet and breakdancing. It all seemed very un-Swiss, but it worked. A range of aromatic Swatches (smelling of strawberry, banana, or mint) launched in 1984 accounted for 80% of all watch sales in the United States in the first two months of 1985. Not only did Ivan Lendl wear a Swatch, so did Princess Diana, and she wore two. (Why not, if telling the time was only an incidental benefit of owning one?) The Swatch was on its way to becoming a legend.

Creating a legend, however, had required a great deal of Swiss efficiency, huge capital investment, and an unexpected innovative spirit. It had also required tight control of distribution. Although the distribution policy in America (where the watches were sold in department stores) was different from Europe (where most were sold by traditional jewelers), the company held tightly to certain principles. It reined back production to create a certain rarity value, and no discounting was allowed by any distributor. In addition, counterfeiters were pursued vigorously, each new Swatch model being protected by copyright.

Perhaps most important of all, the quality of the product was excellent. Despite being irreparable, Swatches rarely broke down. Their designs were almost invariably superb: original yet fashionable. Swatches soon became collectibles, with a lively secondary market in the rarer models growing up around the world. Their place in marketing history is secure.

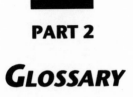

PART 2

GLOSSARY

ABC

See **AUDIT BUREAU OF CIRCULATION**

A/B/C1

A classification used for differential social groups (see **SOCIAL GRADING**). Although A/B/C1 originated in the United Kingdom, it has been exported to other countries through the international influence of U.K. advertising agencies.

ABOVE-THE-LINE

The part of a company's marketing budget that is spent on **ADVERTISING** in the **MEDIA** as opposed to the portion spent on activities such as sales promotion and **DIRECT MARKETING**, which are (emotively and much to the disgust of their practitioners) described as below-the-line.

The line metaphor probably originates in accounting terminology. Marketers increasingly talk of "crossing the line" when referring to their attempts to create integrated communications.

ACCOUNT DIRECTOR

The top manager in an advertising agency; within the agency, the person in charge of a team responsible for an account (a client). Each client has a team, and each team has an account director.

The account director coordinates the various functions represented in a typical team — for example, **CREATIVE, MEDIA,** and **MARKETING RESEARCH.** Depending on the size of the agency and on the size of the client, the account director may work with an account manager who is responsible for day-to-day liaison between the client and the various departments within the agency.

ACHIEVER

A category of American consumer from the widely used VALS classification (see also LIFESTYLE).

ACTION PLAN

A blow-by-blow description of the tactics devised to achieve a particular strategy. An action plan includes schedules of what has to be done when, how, and by whom.

In MARKETING, an action plan should typically include the following:

- Times and places of specific promotions of the PRODUCT (for example, special sample offers, point-of-sale displays, or coupons)
- Trade shows to be attended
- Advertising campaigns to be launched
- Publicity releases to be distributed

It should also include a budget for each type of promotion.

Adidas shoes are named after their founder, a German called Adolf Dassler. Adolf was known to his friends as Adi Das-sler. Despite being an abbreviation of a proper name, the trademark is always spelled with a lower case "a": adidas.

ADOPTION

The process by which consumers adopt a new PRODUCT, fashion, or idea. Adoption can happen only after consumers have passed through various stages:

- Awareness. Consumers are first made aware of the new product's existence.
- Interest. Consumers' interest in the product is titillated by advertising and promotion.

- Evaluation. Consumers evaluate the product in relation to their own needs and desires.
- Trial. Consumers have been hooked enough to go out and try the product.
- Adoption. Consumers continue to buy the product regularly.

ADVERTISING

A key part of MARKETING, but far from being (as is often assumed) the sum total of it. Advertising is the use of MEDIA to inform consumers about something and/or to persuade them to do something.

Communication is a central part of the advertising business, but the industry has not been very successful at communicating its own value. It is widely criticized for creating illusory desires in consumers to the sole benefit of industrial corporations.

There is a contradiction in the general public's attitude to advertising. On the one hand it is seen as manipulative and cunning (as in subliminal advertising); on the other hand it is seen as unfocused and crude. It can, of course, be both — but not at the same time.

Most professional advertising is not haphazard. Different approaches and different messages are required for different stages of the relationship between consumer and PRODUCT. These stages make up the HIERARCHY OF EFFECTS:

- Awareness
- Knowledge
- Liking
- Preference
- Conviction
- Purchase

They are also commonly remembered by the mnemonic AIDA (attention, interest, desire, action).

Advertising is not solely concerned with commercial products. In most countries producers of goods and services account for about half of all advertising expenditure. The other half is spent by marketing intermediaries (such as retailers and wholesalers), by governments in all their guises, by service organizations (such as charities), and by individuals (in a classified advertisement, for example).

Advertising is the most fun you can have with your clothes on.

Jerry Della Femina, advertising agency founder

ADVERTISING AGENCY

A firm that handles the advertising needs of a number of clients. The agency is an intermediary between the producer of goods or services and the MEDIA that will communicate the producer's message to the consumer.

A typical modern agency will have a number of different departments.

- Research. To provide MARKETING RESEARCH relevant to the agency's clients. Data on market behavior will be gathered either from secondary sources or from specially commissioned surveys carried out on behalf of the client. Some agencies are part of a group within which there is also a marketing research firm to keep such survey work within the corporate "family."

- Planning. To give specialist marketing advice to the generalist account director. In some agencies the planning department is merged with the research department.

- CREATIVE. The place where bright new advertising ideas are supposed to be fermented.

- MEDIA. Responsible for planning advertising schedules and for buying space in the media.

- Production. Concerned with the making of all material for television, film, or radio, and for the production of ready-to-print press advertising material. Smaller agencies subcontract much of their production outside the firm, but most bigger agencies have their own full-fledged production departments.

- TRAFFIC. This is sometimes called the control department and is responsible for seeing that each stage of the production process is completed on schedule. Its deadlines are created by publication dates or by broadcast transmission times.

- Accounting. Similar to accounting departments in most commercial firms. It is responsible for BILLING clients and for paying freelance artists, photographers, and writers.

One agency's advice on how best to use an agency is as follows:

- Provide it with a clear and practical brief.
- Establish a clear and workable budget.
- Provide a realistic timetable.
- Carefully check the agency's copy, artwork, and so on.
- Have a clear and realistic business objective against which the agency's work can be measured.

ADVERTISING CAMPAIGN

A coordinated series of advertisements appearing over a defined period of time and in one or more media. An advertising campaign aims to obtain the maximum influence on a TARGET MARKET for a given amount of money.

Your advertising will be made ineffective by bad performance anywhere else: from poor product to dire distribution.

Robert Heller

ADVERTISING/SALES RATIO (A/S)

The total expenditure on **ADVERTISING** in a period expressed as a percentage of the total sales for the period. The a/s ratio can be applied to a **BRAND**, a company, even a whole industry, and is widely used as a yardstick for deciding on advertising budgets.

ADVERTISING STANDARDS

The potential for advertisers to put out material that is misleading, or even downright dishonest, is a continual problem for governments and regulatory authorities. The maintenance of high standards in **ADVERTISING** is usually left, first, to the advertising industry itself.

In most developed countries the industry sets out a code of behavior rich in words such as "legal," "decent," "honest," and "truthful." Behind them is the general principle that advertisements should not mislead, misrepresent, or offend.

In many countries films and television commercials are vetted by a regulatory authority before they are shown. Press advertising is ultimately controlled by the ability of the public to complain about it. By definition that almost always occurs after the event, in other words when the damage is done. In the United States the Federal Trade Commission judges whether advertising is unfair or deceptive.

Although blatant cases of misleading advertising are rare nowadays, occasional examples still creep through. The most notorious recent case was the advertisement for Volvo cars in which a Volvo was seen to resist being crushed by a huge digger, while competitors' models were squashed to pieces. What the advertisement did not show was that the Volvo had been specially reinforced and the competitors' models had been specially weakened.

Complaints most often focus on the decency aspect of advertisements. Benetton has been a notorious offender. Advertisements promoting its range of women and children's wear have used a photograph of a man dying of AIDS and one of a nun affectionately kissing a monk. Perhaps the most shocking aspect of the ads has been their success in increasing Benetton's sales. Nevertheless there is some debate as to whether this sort of shock advertising helps or hurts in the long term.

When business is good it pays to advertise.
When business is bad you've got to advertise.

Anon

ADVERTORIAL

Most manufacturers agree that the best ADVERTISING in newspapers and magazines for their products is flattering copy in the editorial sections of the publication. A major part of the job of PUBLIC RELATIONS is to encourage such copy.

Failing that, some companies try to make their advertisements look like editorials — hence the term "advertorial." Some publishers may allow such advertorials to appear; others will demand that the copy have the word "Advertisement" printed clearly at the top; and still others will insist that the advertisement use a different typeface from that used for the publication's normal editorial matter.

AFTER-SALES SERVICE

A service provided by a manufacturer to a consumer after the consumer has bought the manufacturer's product. After-sales service has been publicly significant in the MARKETING of consumer durables like washing machines, heating systems, and personal computers. It includes things like regular checkups, repairs, supplying spare parts, and so on. Such a service may be provided under the terms of a specific maintenance agreement (separate from the purchase) for which the consumer pays an annual fee.

AIDA

Probably the oldest mnemonic in marketing, AIDA describes the stepping stones to successful communication:

- Get *A*ttention
- Hold *I*nterest
- Arouse *D*esire
- Obtain *A*ction

Alligators? Just floating handbags really.

Copywriter

ALTERNATE DEMAND

A term taken from economics that refers to the demand for products that can be substituted for each other, for example: tea and coffee as drinks; buses and trains as transport; gas and electricity as heating fuel; magazines and television as home entertainment.

Marketers evaluating existing competition for their products must look not only at manufacturers of similar products but also at any alternate demand.

The Alfa-Romeo car got its name because an Italian called Nicola Romeo was once manager of a company called Societá Anonima Lombarda Fabbrica Automobili. The car that Mr. Romeo's company produced should (strictly) have been known as the Salfa-Romeo.

AMA

See AMERICAN MARKETING ASSOCIATION

AMERICAN MARKETING ASSOCIATION

The American Marketing Association (AMA) is the leading association of marketing managers and teachers in the United States. Founded in 1936, it has chapters all over the country and sponsors a number of annual conferences. It publishes several journals with wide international circulation. The oldest, the *Journal of Marketing*, dates back to the end of the nineteenth century.

ANIMAL TESTING

The testing of household products or medicines on animals before the products are sold to humans. Some countries impose a legal requirement that certain potentially harmful substances be so tested before they can be consumed by homo sapiens.

Animal testing is on the decline. The activities of antivivisection groups and the success of companies (like The Body Shop) that make a point of avoiding it have persuaded even cosmetics giants like Revlon and Avon to stop testing on animals.

ANIMATIC

A rough commercial made from a STORYBOARD.

ATOMISTIC TEST

The separate testing of individual elements of the DESIGN of a new advertisement or packaging. For example, in an advertisement for Levi's jeans the JINGLE might be tried out on an audience separately from the look of the male model wearing the jeans, or of the female model looking at the male model who is wearing the jeans. A holistic test tests all these elements together.

ATTITUDES

The collection of beliefs and feelings that together influence a consumer's buying behavior. The factors that go toward determining attitudes are complex. Marketing specialists try to understand them in order to present products in a favorable light or to change attitudes through so-called attitude management.

This is not easy. How, for example, can you convince somebody who firmly believes that Japanese cars are unbeatable value for money to buy a BMW? Similarly, can the proud patriot ever be attracted by a foreign car?

When Honda first decided to introduce its motorcycles into the American market, it faced a hostile attitude toward the PRODUCT: motorcycles were seen as dangerous and associated with violent gangs. However, with ADVERTISING based on the slogan "You meet the nicest people on a Honda," the Japanese company succeeded in changing many people's attitudes toward the motorcycle in general, and to Honda's motorcycle in particular.

ATTRIBUTES

The characteristics of a PRODUCT that are important to consumers. For example, aroma, flavor, caffeine content, and price are the main attributes of instant coffee; flavor, color, smell, thickness, saltiness, and texture are the attributes of chicken soup.

Marketers try to describe products in terms of their attributes: instant coffees may have "an aroma of freshly percolated coffee," while chicken soups are "thick and chunky" or "like mother used to make."

Different consumers weigh the importance of a product's attributes differently, particularly consumers living in different regions.

AUDIENCE RESEARCH

The process of measuring and analyzing radio and television audiences. The size and the composition of such audiences are basic bread-and-butter information for the marketing manager and **ADVERTISING AGENCY**, as are the circulation figures of newspapers and magazines. (See **AUDIT BUREAU OF CIRCULATION**)

National television audience measurement is undertaken by **A. C. NIELSEN**, a company that prepares the definitive Nielsen Television Index (NTI) and the Nielsen Audience Composition (NAC). Surveys of local television audiences are done by the American Research Bureau (ARB). ARB also provides data on radio audiences.

Any attempt to measure TV audiences is dogged by a problem that the printed media never hesitate to point out. Audience research can measure the number of television sets that are actually switched on and the channel that they are switched on to. It cannot take account of the fact that many television sets are switched on but unwatched. Many so-called viewers are asleep, in another room, or engaged in conversation.

AUDIT

A survey of the sales of a **PRODUCT** at different retail outlets, by price, size, and the like. Such surveys are carried out by a number of research companies (the best known is **A. C. NIELSEN**) and are often commissioned by a syndicate of manufacturers in the same industrial sector. The data gathered usually cover a one-month period.

The development of **EPOS** and laser scanning has improved the ability of researchers to produce ever more sophisticated audits.

AUDIT BUREAU OF CIRCULATION

Many countries around the world have a national organization bearing this name. Commonly known as ABC, the Audit Bureau of Circulation publishes regular audited statements of newspapers' and magazines' circulation figures. These are eagerly analyzed by advertisers who need to know how many readers they are reaching and at what cost (see **COST PER MILLE**).

In the United States ABC is sponsored by national and local advertisers as well as by advertising agencies and publishers.

AWARENESS

The ability of individuals to remember a particular advertisement. Awareness is measured in two ways:

1. Aided. The individual is asked a question such as, "Have you heard of an instant coffee called Maxwell House?"

2. Unaided (or spontaneous). The individual is asked a question such as, "Can you name a brand of instant coffee?"

Measures of awareness are widely used as indicators of the effectiveness of marketing strategies.

BABY BOOMERS

The generation of consumers — 76 million strong in the United States — born between 1946 and 1964. In most developed countries there was a pronounced upward blip in the birth rate in those years. Because of their numbers and their purchasing power, baby boomers have been studied closely by marketers. They are a generation that has had to redefine the meaning of "hard times."

The baby boomers themselves gave birth to another blip in the population in the 1980s as they had children of their own. A big marketing issue for the future is how the baby boomers will behave when they become EMPTY NESTERS.

BAIT AND SWITCH

An illegal marketing practice in which a RETAILER (or advertiser) "baits" customers into wanting to purchase something (by, say, offering it very cheaply) and then makes them "switch" their purchase to a more profitable item. For example, customers are persuaded to switch when retailers say they have run out of the advertised product (which they had no intention of selling in the first place).

BANDED PACK

A sales promotion device similar to a QUANTITY DISCOUNT. Two or more items of the same PRODUCT are bound together as a single pack and offered for sale at a price that is less than the combined price of the items sold singly.

Banded packs include familiar offers such as "three for the price of two" or "buy two and get a third free." They are frequently used for selling such items as bars of soap or tubes of toothpaste.

After World War II both the Americans and the British were offered the Volkswagen "Beetle" design by the Germans. The U.K.'s Lord Rootes said: "The vehicle does not meet the fundamental requirements of a motor car. To build the car commercially would be a completely uneconomic enterprise." The Americans were more blunt. One senior executive said to his boss: "Mr. Ford, I don't think what we are being offered here is worth a damn."

The Beetle went on to become one of the most successful car designs of all time.

BAR CODE

A series of lines of varying thickness printed on the side of a PRODUCT or its label. Now familiar in many countries, bar coding allows an electronic scanner at the POINT OF SALE to read automatically certain information about the product, including its price. This speeds up the checkout process and enables vendors to keep a tighter control on inventory and to spot new patterns in their sales.

BARGAIN BASEMENT

This term once referred to the basement of a DEPARTMENT STORE, where merchandise was traditionally sold off at discounted prices. Department stores find other uses for their basements these days, but the expression endures: "bargain-basement prices" are prices that cannot be beaten.

BELONGER

One category in a well-known U.S. classification of consumers. (See LIFESTYLE)

BENEFIT SEGMENTATION

The division of a **MARKET** into groups of consumers who are looking for the same benefit from a **PRODUCT**. For example, one segment of the toothpaste market consists of those who are chiefly concerned with preventing tooth decay (Crest's target market); another contains those consumers whose primary concern is the whiteness and brightness of their teeth.

BIG TICKET ITEM

The sort of big purchases that consumers often make on credit; for example, cars or washing machines. The **MARKETING** of such items demands greater emphasis on ancillary services, such as credit terms, **AFTER-SALES SERVICE**, guarantees, and so on.

BILLBOARD

Literally, boards on which to stick bills (that is, advertisements — as in "bill of fare"). Billboards are usually large, visible, and close to major roads and highways. On them are placed **POSTERS**, illuminated signs, or even samples of the product being advertised. In some countries billboards are controlled strictly by law; in others the controls are lax, especially (as is often the case) when the billboards are owned by local governments, which make large profits from renting them out to advertisers with little incentive to keep them sightly.

I think that I shall never see
A billboard lovely as a tree.
Indeed unless the billboards fall
I'll never see a tree at all.

Ogden Nash

BILLINGS

A measure of the size of an **ADVERTISING AGENCY**. Advertising agencies are paid a percentage of the amount that it costs to put their clients' advertisements in the **MEDIA**. Called the advertiser's billings, this cost gives a rough idea of the amount of business that an agency is doing.

BIODEGRADABLE

The ability of a **PRODUCT** to be broken down naturally — that is, by the forces of nature. Leave a biodegradable product in the ground for some time and it will not exist in any recognizable form. Leaves, bananas, and paper packaging are all biodegradable.

In today's environmentally conscious marketing, biodegradable is a valuable **ATTRIBUTE** of a **BRAND**. Consumers feel good about buying biodegradable packaging, for example.

Birds Eye, the frozen foods advertised around the world by the seafaring Cap'n Birdseye, were indeed named after a real Mr. Birdseye. Clarence (known as "Bob") Birdseye (1886–1956) invented a process for freezing food in packages small enough to be sold retail. The idea came to him on a trip to the Arctic.

BLIND TEST

A marketing research technique in which two unidentified products are sampled by consumers who indicate their preference. Blind testing is often used in new product research to test the product against an established **BRAND**.

Because brand names and packaging heavily influence consumers' perception of products, blind testing is the only way to measure factors such as taste, smell, and texture on a comparative basis. In some blind tests, for example, Australian wines have been preferred to French wines by people who in general consider French wines to be superior.

Blind testing is a familiar feature of television commercials, in which by law a test must be genuine. A series of commercials called the Pepsi Challenge claimed that a majority of people preferred Pepsi to Coca-Cola and helped Pepsi raise its profile in markets where Coke is synonymous with cola. But the fact of the matter is that neither cola nor anything else is sold under blind-test conditions. On the shelf, Pepsi has to compete with the Coca-Cola brand name.

In the United States Coke has about 45% of the soft drink market, Pepsi about 30%.

BLISTER PACK

A form of packaging in which products are wrapped in clear plastic (or with a transparent window) so that consumers can properly see what they are buying before they buy it.

BLOW-UP

A greatly enlarged photograph used in a marketing presentation. It is not greatly different from a "beauty shot": a close-up picture of a product.

BLURB

The short piece of copy that appears on the jacket or inside cover of a book. Hence any short piece of copy that praises something extravagantly.

See how glamorous acronyms can become when divorced from their original connotations. BMW stands for Bayerische Motoren Werke: the Bavarian Motor Works.

BODY COPY

The main text in a piece of marketing material, as opposed to the headlines or the details in footnotes.

BODY LANGUAGE

A means of nonverbal communication expressed through movements of the body. Much television advertising uses body language to express emotions: quicker and easier than using words, it is also universal. Much body language is common to peoples in the East, the West, the North, and the South. But be careful: nodding the head up and down means "yes" in some cultures and "no" in others.

BRAND

According to **PHILIP KOTLER**, author of *Marketing Management*, the world's standard marketing textbook, a brand is "a name, term, symbol, or design (or a combination of them) which is intended to signify the goods or services of one seller or group of sellers and to differentiate them from those of competitors." When marketed successfully, a brand becomes a powerful force in the marketplace; Hoover, Mars, Kleenex, and Levi's, for example, instantly identify products familiar to everyone. In markets where famous brands exist, competitors are always at a disadvantage.

Brands may be used in various ways.

- Family brands are product names which all contain the name of the company: Heinz Tomato Ketchup, Heinz Baked Beans, and so on.

- Individual brands stand alone. Procter & Gamble's products all carry individual brand names, for instance, Tide, Ivory, Pampers.

- Some companies use different brand names for different product lines: Sears, Roebuck, for example, sells appliances under the brand name Kenmore and tools under the brand name Craftsman.

- Sometimes the brand name is attached to a company or divisional name. This is known as an umbrella brand, and is used to endorse the product, while at the same time allowing it to develop its own brand personality.

- Brands can also be owned by intermediate agents (see **DEALER BRAND**) or by manufacturers (see **MANUFACTURER BRAND**).

- Brands can be people as well as things. Madonna is a brand; so is Tom Cruise; and so (to her eternal bemusement) was Marilyn Monroe.

The word "brand" has been around for a long time. It is derived from an old Norse word, *brandr*, which means "to burn"; hence the "branding" of livestock.

BRAND EQUITY VALUATION

The process of attaching a value to a company's brands. That brands have considerable value is beyond question. When Philip Morris bought the Kraft food company in 1988, it paid $12.9 billion. That was four times the value of Kraft's tangible assets; in other words, Philip Morris paid just short of $10 billion for intangible assets. Most of them were the brands that Kraft had developed over the years: its own-name range of products plus things like Miracle Whip and Breyers ice cream. The Kraft exchange and similar purchases at about that time alerted companies to the fact that brands might be a significant intangible asset.

But how can you determine what these numbers should be? A U.K. firm called Interbrand has developed a brand-value calculation formula that is as good as any. It takes an objective measure of the brand's recent profitability and multiplies it by a number (maximum 20) based on a subjective judgment of seven different aspects of the brand:

- Its leadership (or otherwise) in its MARKET.
- Its stability (or longevity).
- The nature of the market. Is it large and stable (like food and drink) or subject to fast-changing fashion (like green hair dye)?
- Its internationality: international brands are assumed to have more strength (both domestically and abroad) than purely national brands.
- The trend for the brand.
- The marketing support for the brand.
- Its protection in law: as a registered TRADEMARK, PATENT, and so on.

The aspects are weighted; see the following table for examples (figures are %).

	Maximum	Kellogg's	Budweiser
Leadership	25	22	18
Stability	15	14	12
Market	10	8	8
Internationality	25	22	15
Trend	10	8	7
Support	10	8	8
Protection	5	5	3
Total	100	87	71

BRAND IMAGE

The aura behind a particular brand. In his book *World Class Brands*, Chris Macrae developed a typology of brands. In it there are five main categories:

1. The ritual brand. Associated with special occasions such as

champagne for a wedding, cranberry sauce for a Thanksgiving dinner.

2. The symbol brand. For example, the famous Lacoste Izod alligator or McDonald's arches. The symbol is the value; what it is attached to is almost irrelevant.

3. The "heritage of good" brand. This is usually the first brand to establish itself as providing specific benefits: Kellogg's for a bright start to the day; The Body Shop for how to have an environmentally clean conscience, painless feet, and no wrinkles.

4. Belonging brands. These give the consumer a feeling of belonging to a group. For example, Marlboro smokers, who are all macho cowboys at heart (although when Marlboro was first launched they were all smart city women); or wearers of Benetton clothes, who are all members of a multiracial, multicolored global village.

5. The legend. For example, the Levi 501 jean (the first ever made by the company) or the Porsche Carrera, or Nike's Air Jordans, named for Michael Jordan.

BRAND LOYALTY

The aim of all brand managers is to secure the sustained loyalty of consumers to their particular **PRODUCT**. Brand loyalty comes about through consumers' continued satisfaction with the product and through effective and often heavy promotion. Brand loyalty is not just sustained repurchase of a brand, but is a strong commitment to that brand.

Strong brand loyalty reduced the impact of **ADVERTISING** by competitive brands and discourages brand switching.

BRAND MANAGEMENT

Also known as **PRODUCT MANAGEMENT**. A management system developed in the 1930s by Procter & Gamble, it has grown into a widely accepted method of managing individual brands in multiproduct companies.

A brand manager is given responsibility for a single BRAND and becomes that product's champion and enthusiast within the company. He or she sets the brand's marketing objectives, plans what action is needed to achieve these objectives (such as target market identification, ADVERTISING, sales promotion, packaging, and so on), schedules and coordinates all the marketing activities, and reports to the product group management.

Most companies using this P&G system of brand management treat the brand manager's domain as a PROFIT CENTER.

Brand management is an ideal training ground for future marketing directors, and jobs as assistant brand managers are usually in great demand. The brand management system is changing today to a system of product category management. Under this new brand-management system, the strategy for the whole product line is coordinated.

BROWN GOODS

A somewhat outdated term describing consumer durables formerly encased in brown veneer: old-fashioned radios and televisions in cabinets, and record players, for example. Brown goods were usually contrasted with WHITE GOODS.

Most of today's white goods are still encased in white, but brown goods now appear more often in black or in shades of gray. Hence the expression has fallen into disuse.

BUNDLING

The process of offering services related to a PRODUCT at a special price to those who purchase the product. For example, software packages are often bundled with the purchase of computer hardware. Banks bundle free checking accounts or free safe-deposit services to those who maintain high average balances in their accounts.

Leo Burnett

One of the ten biggest advertising agency groups in the world. A folksy firm with some folksy creations such as the Jolly Green Giant. Like **YOUNG & RUBICAM**, but unlike most agencies, it eschewed the stock market in the 1980s, remaining a private company with a carefully tended list of blue-chip clients. Half of its big clients have been with the agency for more than 20 years.

Its strategy seemed to pay off in the early 1990s as it gleaned more new business during the recession than any other major agency.

Business-to-business advertising

Sometimes called industrial advertising. Most **ADVERTISING** is directed at individual consumers, but a significant segment is produced by businesses for businesses. Manufacturers of machine tools or construction equipment, for example, do not market their products to individuals for their own use, but for the use of their companies.

Specialist trade journals and trade fairs are very important media for these companies and for business-to-business advertising in general. (In the United States there are almost three times as many specialist trade journals as consumer magazines.)

Buyer's market

Any market in which supply exceeds demand. Such a market can arise either because the supply of a **PRODUCT** has been increased by a number of new entrants into the market or because the demand for the product has declined as recession or changing consumer tastes have hit the market. Either way, buyers will force down prices in such a market until supply is cut by a reduction in the number of suppliers.

*What good is the moon if you can't buy it
or sell it?*

Ivan Boesky, financier, 1986

BUYGRID

A widely used model of industrial buying, which identifies three
different types of situation.

1. New task. The situation that occurs when an organization
   has no previous experience of the task in hand.
2. Modified rebuy. The situation in which an organization re-
   assesses its position, perhaps searching for quality improvements and cost reductions. Such a reassessment is usually
   triggered by some dissatisfaction with existing suppliers or
   the entry of new suppliers.
3. Straight rebuy. The situation that requires little reassessment and largely entails reordering from current suppliers.

BUYING CYCLE

The frequency with which products are purchased. The buying
cycle for bread is a matter of days, for sugar a matter of weeks,
and for cars a matter of years.

CANNIBALIZATION

When increased sales of one **BRAND** result in decreased sales of another within the same **PRODUCT LINE**. Cannibalization is a danger when products or brands in a company's product line are insufficiently differentiated or when competition among a company's brand managers becomes too intense (see **BRAND MANAGEMENT**).

There is always a risk of cannibalization when a company extends a product line. For example, when powder-based detergents were first marketed in liquid form there was a danger that the extension brand (the liquid detergent) would reduce sales of the original powdered brand to such an extent that the combined sales (of powder and liquid) were less than the sales of the original powder on its own.

CAPTIVE MARKET

A group of consumers that has no choice. This may be either because products (or services) are provided by a monopoly supplier (like telecommunications services in most countries) or because the consumers are in a particular situation that does not allow them choice, for example, the food and drink in a movie theater.

CASCADING

A marketing strategy, favored by the Japanese, in which a small well-defined market segment is penetrated first before the manufacturer "cascades" into other markets. For example, Honda started in the United States with the **MARKETING** of small motorcycles; it is now a major importer of automobiles into the United States.

The benefit of such a strategy is that an initial entry into a narrowly focused market provokes little competition. That enables the marketer to build up a distribution and servicing network without attracting too much attention.

CASH AND CARRY

A form of limited-service wholesaling that has become popular in various sectors since the 1960s. Cash-and-carry shops are like wholesale warehouses (taking delivery in bulk from manufacturers). The RETAILER or customer gets minimal service. There is no sales force, no delivery service, no credit, no reordering assistance; in short, no frills. The retailer or customer goes to the warehouse, pays for the goods, and takes them away. It means lower costs to the WHOLESALER and lower prices to the retailer.

The success of the cash-and-carry concept owed much to changing patterns of consumer shopping. As shoppers turned more and more to huge supermarket chains, the only way that smaller independent retailers (like corner groceries or village stores) could compete was by cutting costs to the bone. That included buying from the cash-and-carry chains.

Small hotels and restaurants also rely heavily on cash-and-carry outlets.

CATALOGUE STORE

Such a store combines the benefits of catalogue selling with those of the BARGAIN BASEMENT. It deals in such national brand products as jewelry, appliances, luggage, watches, and hi-fi equipment. Customers who come to the store view the goods and then order them from catalogues. The inventory is stored behind the catalogue showroom, and customers' orders are brought out to them. Customer comfort is not a first priority: lines may form both for ordering and for collecting goods. Prices, however, are discounted and are very competitive.

CATI

See **COMPUTER-ASSISTED TELEPHONE INTERVIEWING**

CAVEAT EMPTOR

Latin for "let the buyer beware," a phrase that had great legal significance in the days before the spate of modern laws designed to protect the consumer. In the absence of an express guarantee in a contract, buyers purchased goods at their own risk.

Today's consumers are protected by laws both with respect to the manufacture of products (through implied warranties) and with respect to the retailing of them. For example, goods bought from retailers must correspond with their description (be what they are said to be). They must also be of "merchantable quality" and be fit for their purpose (do what they are meant to do).

CENTRAL BUYING

Each outlet in **DEPARTMENT STORE** or **SUPERMARKET** chains does not necessarily purchase its own merchandise. Buying may be done centrally at a head office, and the merchandise is distributed by the head office around the chain.

Such central buying is done in order to make economies of scale; the head office can get bigger discounts for buying in greater bulk, and fewer people are required to do the same amount of buying.

CHAIN STORE

A store belonging to a group of retail outlets that are linked in one of three possible ways.

1. Corporate chains. These consist of retail outlets owned and managed by one company. The chains have a central buying office and centrally managed **MARKETING, ADVERTISING**, and **MERCHANDISING**.

The corporate chain was pioneered by F.W. Woolworth, which opened its first store in the United States in 1879. Nowadays the grocery business is increasingly dominated by chain stores such as Safeway and Wal-Mart.

2. Voluntary association chains. These are groups of independent retailers that gather themselves around a single **WHOLESALER** such as IGA.

3. Franchises. The fastest-growing retail chains in many countries in recent years have been franchise operations like McDonald's, Benetton, Pizza Hut, and so on.

CHANNEL CAPTAIN

Whoever is the most powerful member of the channel of **DISTRIBUTION** (from manufacturer to **WHOLESALER** to **RETAILER**) is known as the channel captain. Traditionally, the channel captain has been a manufacturer. In the car industry, companies like General Motors have tended to dominate their dealer networks.

But there have always been retailers who have been channel captains. The Limited has built up such a position for itself in very little time. The Limited's own manufacturers feed its 3,800 stores, and it controls a bank that provides credit to divisions within the company as well as credit cards to its customers.

CHANNEL CONFLICT

Disagreement between members of a **DISTRIBUTION CHANNEL**. Such conflict can be either horizontal or vertical.

• Horizontal channel conflict occurs among retailers going head to head when one **RETAILER** feels that another is competing too strongly, or is invading its territory unacceptably with its advertising.

• Vertical channel conflict occurs between retailers and their suppliers (manufacturers) when either side feels itself unduly dominated by the other.

When Chevrolet introduced a new car called the Nova into the Mexican market, it forgot that in Spanish no va means "it does not go."

CIRCULATION AND READERSHIP

Circulation is the average number of people who receive each issue of a newspaper or magazine; it is a number closely watched by advertisers who want to reach a certain size of audience, and it is audited (to make sure that publishers do not cheat) by organizations like the **AUDIT BUREAU OF CIRCULATION**.

Readership is a slightly different concept. It is the number of individuals who read each copy of a publication. Whereas something like a cheap local daily newspaper will be read by only one person (the purchaser), more expensive and longer-lasting magazines will be read over their lifetime by several people (especially if they are left in the waiting rooms of doctors or dentists).

The total number of people who read a publication is the circulation multiplied by the average number of readers of a copy.

CLASSIFIED ADVERTISEMENT

Small advertisements of a few lines, often written without professional help, that appear in certain newspapers and magazines. Classifieds advertise real estate for sale or rent, help wanted or available, cars, pets and pet supplies, and second-hand household goods.

Each classified advertisement is relatively cheap, but added together they can become a significant source of revenue for a publication. Some publications contain nothing but classified ads and are purchased only for the purpose of shopping for something.

CLUSTER ANALYSIS

A statistical technique that sorts a SAMPLE into a number of groups (or clusters) that have features in common.

Coca-Cola, the most famous brand name in the world, was formed in 1886 out of the names of two of its ingredients: extract of coca leaves and cola nuts.

COGNITIVE DISSONANCE

The anxiety that a consumer experiences after making a significant purchase. The consumer will initially consider the positive attributes of the item not chosen along with the negative attributes of the item actually purchased. To relieve this anxiety, the consumer will then attempt to focus on the positive attributes of the item he or she has purchased.

COLD CALLING

Calling on a customer without a prior appointment. Many retail businesses expect salespeople to drop in regularly and unexpectedly. For many kinds of selling, however, cold calling is unwelcome, inefficient, and time-wasting. Where it is unavoidable, the hit rate (the proportion of calls that are converted into actual sales) is very low.

COLOR

The power of color in establishing a BRAND should not be underestimated. Different colors mean different things: red is universally considered to be warm, blue is generally cold. But the significance of colors is also culturally determined. Certain yellows and oranges that the Japanese appreciate, for example, do not have the same impact in Europe.

A product's color can become a valuable asset. Marlboro's red and IBM's blue are recognized colors in many a printer's spectrum. The strength of a **PROMOTION** may be greatly diminished if a printer does not reproduce the precise color associated with a brand.

Communication takes place in the ear of the listener, not in the mouth of the speaker.

Anon

COMMUNICATIONS STRATEGY

The choice of different ways in which marketers set out to communicate with their markets: often a combination of direct face-to-face communication between a **SALESPERSON** and a potential customer, and indirect nonpersonal communication through **ADVERTISING** and sales promotion.

The nature of a **PRODUCT** and of its **MARKET** influences a company's communications strategy. If its products are targeted at mass consumer markets, and if the company can afford it, then its communications strategy need consist of nothing more than a strong dose of media advertising.

On the other hand, industrial marketing generally calls for personal selling to meet the often highly specialized needs of industrial customers.

Communications is the most important form of marketing.

Akio Morita, chairman of Sony

COMPARATIVE ADVERTISING

The controversial practice of advertising a product by comparing it — to its advantage — with its competitors. This goes beyond the old practice of comparing the advertiser's product with an anonymous Brand X. All brands are named.

Comparative advertising can be very effective, but it is potentially litigious. One unsupported bit of knocking copy about the competition, and the lawsuits can fall as fast as the sales chart.

COMPUTER-ASSISTED TELEPHONE INTERVIEWING

Computer-assisted telephone interviewing (CATI) is conducted by an interviewer using a computer and a computerized questionnaire. The interviewer reads the questions from the computer's visual display unit and keys in the respondents' answers. Since the computer can follow complex questionnaire routing very efficiently (for example, "If the answer to Question 10 is No, then go to Question 15"), interviewer errors are much reduced. The processing of data is also very much faster.

Man — Slow, Slovenly, Brilliant
IBM — Fast, Accurate, Stupid

Sign in IBM Tokyo office

CONCENTRATED SEGMENTATION

Some companies, particularly smaller ones, identify a comparatively small segment of a MARKET on which to concentrate their marketing effort. By selecting a niche in the market for themselves, they hope to avoid head-on competition with larger and more powerful rivals.

A classic example of a successful product in a small market is the Rolls-Royce car, which has catered for many years to a small but affluent international market. Another example is the California company that found a niche for itself making personalized buses for rock stars, people who spend much of their lives literally "on the road."

Concentrated segmentation has become better known as **NICHE MARKETING** and has become very fashionable in recent years. It is no guarantee of a safe market haven, however. Mass marketers will ignore niches for only as long as they see no way to compete in them profitably, and they do not feel threatened by them. IBM, for example, entered the cheap personal computer market (under another brand name) because the threat to its personal computer business from a vast range of copy-cat, cut-price manufacturers became too great even for the mighty Big Blue to ignore.

The magazine market is in a state of constant segmentation. In 1988 there were 491 new specialist consumer magazines launched in the United States.

CONCEPT TESTING

A technique used to test new ideas (concepts) at an early stage in the development of a **PRODUCT**. Qualitative research techniques such as **GROUP DISCUSSION** can yield valuable insights into how consumers might perceive a new product idea, how it might be used, when, and by whom. For example, a group of homemakers might be brought together and asked to test the concept of robotic housekeeping.

CONJOINT ANALYSIS

A technique used in **NEW PRODUCT DEVELOPMENT**. A company that wants to introduce a new product has to decide what particular features and qualities to give the product so that it can be positioned properly with respect to its competitors.

Every product has a large number of **ATTRIBUTES**; some of them (and some combinations of them) are more important than others. Conjoint analysis is a technique for testing the strength of the various combinations of features in order to develop the combination that is best liked by consumers.

The skill in conjoint analysis lies in choosing the right combinations. It is no good to simply throw together the most popular attributes. For example, suppose a company is designing a new ice cream. It finds that all elderly people want soft ice cream (and plain flavors), while all young people want very sweet flavors and hard ice cream. If it comes out with a very sweet, soft brand, it should not be surprised to find that nobody buys it.

CONSUMER CREDIT

The granting of credit to individuals for the purchase of consumer goods and services. The too rapid withdrawal of consumer credit (either by an increase in interest rates, or by rationing, which governments have on occasion undertaken) can throw an economy into recession, so dependent are today's Western economies on the supply of consumer credit.

In the marketing of consumer durables in particular, the provision of consumer credit is a crucial element in securing a sale; often it is a crucial element in the profitability of the manufacturer, too. Some consumer goods manufacturers make more profit from financing sales than they do from sales themselves.

CONSUMERISM

In 1962, President Kennedy issued a Consumers' Bill of Rights. It never became law, but its recognition of the consumer's four basic rights triggered a consumer "movement" for the rest of the decade.

1. The right to safety
2. The right to be informed
3. The right to choose
4. The right to be heard

The birth of consumerism marked a swing away from the overwhelming power of manufacturers, advertisers, and retailers. It acknowledged that the level of material wealth in most parts of the United States and Europe was so high that consumers could choose which products to buy, or indeed whether to buy any. Societies were beyond the stage where almost anything that could be produced could be sold.

In some respects Japan's economic miracle was based on an early recognition by Japanese firms of the consumer's newfound power. They recognized that such power would force manufacturers to be much more conscious of quality and price.

Consumerism also marked a switch in the importance of different management disciplines. MARKETING became the crucial skill; gone was the almost total management preoccupation with the efficiency of the production process, and with such things as ergonomics and operations research. The most famous champion of the consumer's cause was Ralph Nader, who began his campaigns in the United States with his pursuit of General Motors and its "unsafe at any speed" Corvair. His campaign led to the enactment of the Traffic and Motor Vehicle Safety Act.

CONSUMER PANEL

See DIARY PANEL

CONSUMER PROFILE

A description of the age, social class, and other characteristics of consumers of a given PRODUCT or BRAND. Drawing up consumer profiles is an essential part of the development of a COMMUNICATIONS STRATEGY and of MARKET SEGMENTATION.

*Des qualités trop supérieures rendent souvent
un homme moins propre à la société. On ne
va pas au marché avec des ingots; on y va avec
de l'argent ou de la petite monnaie.*

*(Qualities too elevated often make a man unfit
for society. We do not take ingots with us to
market; we take silver or small change.)*

Nicholas-Sebastien Chamfort (1741–1794)

CONSUMER PROTECTION

Ways in which consumers are protected from illegal or dangerous practices by manufacturers. Much consumer protection legislation arose as a result of the consumerism movement in the
1960s.

Several agencies in the United States are involved in consumer protection and must be taken into account by companies
planning to market a PRODUCT in that country. They include
the Federal Trade Commission (FTC), the Food and Drug Administration (FDA), the Consumer Products Safety Commission
(CPSC), the Environmental Protection Agency (EPA), and the
Office of Consumer Affairs (OCA).

The magazine *Consumer Reports* is produced by an independent consumer association, in which products are tested and
commented on; both the magazine and the association have an
influence on consumer behavior.

CONTROL

A standard by which other production is measured. For example, quality control is the maintenance of quality at or above a
certain required minimum control level.

CONTROLLED CIRCULATION

When a publication is sent free to a number of targeted readers, it is said to have a controlled circulation. The publication can then tell potential advertisers that they will be reaching a particularly desirable audience (for them). However, there is evidence to suggest that publications received free (and without being solicited) are not read nearly as thoroughly as those that are paid for.

CONVENIENCE STORE

Retail outlets that trade primarily on the appeal of the convenience that they offer to customers. (Convenience is one of the small shop's few weapons with which to fight back against the increasing concentration of food retailing in the hands of big supermarkets.)

Convenience stores have four competitive advantages.

1. They sell products based on a knowledge of local consumer needs.
2. They are open for long hours.
3. They are located near their customers.
4. They are small, allowing quick entry and exit.

COPYRIGHT

The legal protection given to artistic, literary, dramatic, and musical works to prevent their being copied without their creator's agreement. In general such protection lasts for the lifetime of the creator and for 50 years after his or her death.

Copyright also protects things like distinctive logo designs and advertising material. It has been included in a recent international effort to provide greater protection around the world to intellectual property rights. The Berne Convention (set up in 1886) also supposedly gives protection in those many countries that have signed it. But it has no teeth to punish wrongdoers, and no system to arbitrate disputes.

CORPORATE CAMPAIGN

An advertising campaign that is aimed less at selling a particular product or service and more at propagating the good name and image of the company in general.

CORPORATE IDENTITY

The unique characteristics of a corporation together define its identity. These characteristics include obvious things like the design of its offices and the style of its PACKAGING as well as less tangible things like its beliefs and the way it conducts its business.

Wally Olins, a corporate identity consultant, says that an effective identity depends on two things: credibility and consistency. "It must spring from the organization's own roots, its values and behavior, its strengths and its weaknesses. And it must be carefully and consistently expressed."

Corporate identity tells the world — whether actively or by default — just what the corporate strategy is.

Wally Olins

CORPORATE LOGO

A company's emblems: a powerful part of its CORPORATE IDEN-TITY. Logos can become as familiar and as powerful as brand names. When AT&T was forcibly broken up, the courts decided that none of the resulting new companies had the right to use AT&T's logo, a distinctive emblem of a Bell telephone.

COST PER THOUSAND

Also expressed as cost per mille (CPM). CPM is a convenient way of comparing the effectiveness of different MEDIA by calculating how much it costs, using each medium, to reach a potential audience of 1,000 people.

For magazines and newspapers, the CPM is easy to calculate: If the cost of a full-page advertisement in a particular magazine is $10,000 and the circulation of the magazine is 250,000, then the CPM is 10,000 ÷ 250 = $40. For television it is not so simple; both the cost and the size of the audience depend on the time that the advertisement is shown.

CPM is only a first approximation of effectiveness. What matters most to marketers is not the simple cost per thousand people reached, but also the cost per thousand people reached who are potential customers and who notice the marketer's message.

COUNTERTRADE

A form of international trading that gets around the difficulty of one party being short of tradable currency. Particularly popular between Eastern and Western Europe, where the former is frequently short of hard cash.

Countertrade can take several forms.

- Barter. For example, when the former Soviet Union paid for Pepsi-Cola with vodka.

- Compensation deals. Payment is partly in goods and partly in an acceptable currency.

- Counterpurchase. Payment is in currency but only on the understanding that the currency will be used to purchase the buying country's goods.

- Buyback deals. A country exporting (say) a chemical plant or machinery for making television tubes accepts partial payment in the form of output from the factory that it is equipping.

COUPON

A certificate that gives the consumer a price reduction on a specific product. Coupons can be included in print advertising, can be mailed to householders, or they can be enclosed in or printed on a product's packaging.

Coupons are heavily used by consumer-goods manufacturers, despite the fact that their redemption rate is less than 5%. City newspapers often have large shopping sections stuffed with coupon offers in their Thursday and Friday editions. Sunday newspapers, too, frequently include coupon inserts.

Coupons are commonly used to encourage the purchase of a new product. When used to stimulate sales of a mature product, they represent a form of price reduction that is more subtle than straightforward price cutting and less likely to be noticed by competitors.

COVERAGE

The percentage of a TARGET MARKET that has at least one opportunity to see an advertisement during a particular campaign.

Ads are the cave art of the 20th century.

The message of Marshall McLuhan

CPM

See COST PER THOUSAND

First, make yourself a reputation for being a creative genius. Second, surround yourself with partners who are better than you. Third, leave them to get on with it.

David Ogilvy's secrets of success

CREATIVE

The department in an **ADVERTISING AGENCY** involved in coming up with the ideas for advertisements and the artistic fulfillment of them, composed primarily of copywriters and graphic artists.

Behind the expression lies the idea that even in the irreverent world of **ADVERTISING** there are two cultures: art and science, producers and sellers, creators and managers. In this scheme of things most activity in advertising agencies (as elsewhere) arises from a time-consuming but creative resolution of the tension between these opposite poles.

CROSS-SELLING

Placing complementary products close to each other in a store. The hope is that the customer who is tempted to buy one will spot the other and fall for that as well. For example, place women's skirts close to blouses and sweaters, or bacon close to eggs.

CUSTOMER PROFILE

A description of a business's customers in terms of their age, income, education, social habits, and so on.

Newspapers and magazines frequently produce profiles of their readers in order to tell advertisers what sort of person they are reaching by putting an advertisement in the publication.

CUSTOMER SERVICE

Once upon a time it was thought that goods were goods and services were services and never the twain would meet. Nowadays most people realize that there are few services that do not involve some goods — think of all the paper that comes with running a bank account, for example — and even fewer goods that do not involve some sort of service. This service can take a variety of forms.

- **AFTER-SALES SERVICE** such as repairs and replacement and/or a guarantee

- The provision of credit
- Technical advice
- Ease of contact (for example, through toll-free phone numbers)
- Complaint services
- Maintenance
- Information services

In general, the more technologically complicated a PRODUCT, the more important is the service component. In the sale of INDUSTRIAL GOODS and of consumer products such as cars or computers, the service component may be at least as important as the product itself in clinching a sale. Pundits currently agree that the key to competitive advantage in the 1990s will lie in service and the quality of it.

Dagmar

See "DEFINING ADVERTISING GOALS FOR MEASURED ADVERTISING RESULTS"

DAR

See DAY-AFTER RECALL

D'Arcy, Masius, Benton & Bowles

A large advertising agency with a strong international presence and headquarters on New York's Broadway, it is the result of a 1985 merger between two long-running agencies, D'Arcy Mac-Manus & Masius and Benton & Bowles.

The agency is known as DMBB; advertising industry executives' obsession with making brand names out of their surnames has created a rich collection of such acronyms.

Database

An organized set of files that provides a common pool of information for several users. Databases about a company's customers are increasingly being held on computer and maintained by marketing departments. They can include information about both existing and potential customers and their characteristics, their buying methods, and their uses of products and services.

Databases can also include information about competitors and other external variables that should be taken into account when planning strategies.

In an age when information is a key part of a company's ability to provide quality competitive products and services for a targeted market of customers who can benefit from those products and services, the construction and use of relevant databases are critical to success.

*If the 1960s was the decade of mass marketing,
the 1970s of segmentation and line extensions,
and the 1980s of micro-marketing, the 1990s
will be the decade of one-to-one marketing.*

Tom Peters

DATE STAMPING

The marking of over-the-counter drugs and perishable food
products, among others, with a date by which the PRODUCT
should be sold. Date stamping is a legal requirement in many
countries.

DAY-AFTER RECALL

Day-after recall (DAR) is a method of analyzing the impact of
an advertisement by finding out what percentage of people exposed to the ad can remember it on the day after it appeared.

DEALER BRAND

A brand name put on a PRODUCT by a middleman, usually a
RETAILER; for example, Ann Page at the A&P stores. Sometimes
known as "private label" or "distributor brand." The increasing
success of these brands reflects the growing power of big retail
chains.

DECISION CLUSTER

The bringing together by consumers of a number of buying decisions. If they buy a chicken, they may also buy stuffing; if they
buy a pen, they may also buy ink, and so on.

DECISION-MAKING UNIT

In industrial buying, decisions on which suppliers' goods or services to purchase are not made as they are by a single consumer

acting alone. Purchasing decisions are reached by a process of consultation among a number of people.

This group of people is referred to as a decision-making unit (DMU) and needs to be carefully identified by industrial salespeople. Also called the buying center.

Several specific roles have been identified in the typical DMU:

- Buyer: executes the purchase and is typically concerned mostly with price.
- User: uses the PRODUCT, and is concerned first with performance.
- Influencer: the technical expert who provides guidelines for the decision.
- Gatekeeper: controls information flows and access to others.
- Decider: formally authorizes the purchase and is concerned with internal policy aspects of the decision.

Within the computer industry different companies focus their marketing on different groups. IBM, for example, has gone for the deciders. These are people who are not computer literate but who know that they cannot be criticized for opting for such an impressive market leader as IBM. Digital, on the other hand, has gone for the technical experts, whose preference is not satisfied as often as is that of the deciders.

"DEFINING ADVERTISING GOALS FOR MEASURED ADVERTISING RESULTS"

The title of an influential essay written by Russell Colley in 1961, commonly known by the acronym DAGMAR. The essay provided a framework for thinking about an elusive goal: how to measure the effect that advertising has (and thus to find out which advertising expenditure is worthwhile).

To some extent the only measure of advertising's success is increased sales, but that is a long-term achievement. In the short term it is possible to measure changes in AWARENESS and ATTITUDE. These provide clues about the effectiveness of ADVERTISING as consumers move through preliminary stages of foreplay on their way to consummating a purchase. (See also AIDA and the HIERARCHY OF EFFECTS)

DEMARKETING

The process of discouraging consumers from buying or consuming. Governments can demarket cigarettes by requiring that health warnings be printed on every pack. Raising prices or restricting distribution in a form of rationing can also be regarded as demarketing. Another example is public utilities which demarket when they approach capacity.

DEMOGRAPHICS

Facts about the composition of a population (its age, sex, family size, family income, occupation, education, religion, race, nationality, and so on). Demographic analysis reveals important marketing information that affects consumer demand — such things as changes in class structure, family composition, and age profile.

The baby boom of the 1960s provided marketing opportunities for food manufacturers like Heinz and Gerber ("Babies are our only business") and Johnson & Johnson (makers of baby powder). As the birth rate fell and the number of elderly people increased, new opportunities were perceived: Gerber switched to insurance ("Gerber now babies the over-50s"); Johnson & Johnson repositioned its baby powder and shampoo as products for adults as well as children.

The increase in the number of working mothers, the growth of the Hispanic population in the United States, and the polarization of populations into the "haves" and the urban underclass (the "have-nots") are other demographic factors with important marketing implications.

At least as significant are shifting distributions of wealth. In most Western nations the first generation of postwar business creators (and home owners) is dying off and/or passing on its wealth to the next generation, most of whom are in the 45–59 age group.

DENTSU

The Japanese challenge to the domination of world advertising by Anglo-Saxon firms (with a few French ones nibbling at their heels). Dentsu is the largest Japanese advertising agency by far, with clients such as Toyota, Canon, and Japan Air Lines. As these Japanese companies have spread around the world, their agency has followed them and its success has reflected theirs.

Dentsu has formed a number of joint ventures with U.S. and European agencies such as YOUNG & RUBICAM. These are designed to help it bridge the culture gap between European and Japanese consumers.

DEPARTMENT STORE

Stores that are traditionally located in the heart of central shopping areas in large cities or in regional shopping malls in the suburbs, carrying a wide range of PRODUCT CLASSES, typically clothing, home furnishings, and household goods. Department stores also give much attention to display and service. The first department store in the world is alleged to have been Bon Marché, which opened in Paris in 1852.

To support the high rents in these locations, and their heavy staffing, department stores have operated on a high mark-up basis. In recent years many have had to close, reflecting intense competition from both discounters and self-service stores selling similar product categories.

They have also been affected by the decline of the central city shopping area.

DEPTH INTERVIEW

An unstructured interview used for marketing research purposes. Respondents talk freely under prompting and guidance from a researcher, usually a psychologist, who tries to uncover deep or hidden levels of motivation and behavior. Psychological techniques such as word association and sentence or story completion may be used.

Depth interviews require highly skilled interviewers, and that makes them very costly. Nevertheless they are a major tool of **MOTIVATIONAL RESEARCH.**

DERIVED DEMAND

A marketing concept derived from economics. Industrial marketers do not sell directly to consumers but to intermediary manufacturers. The demand for **INDUSTRIAL GOODS** and services is thus "derived" from the demand for the consumer goods that require the intermediary product. Thus the demand for the machinery to make tin cans is derived from the demand for products that are packaged in cans.

DESIGN

There are more than 25 different dictionary definitions of the word "design." In general, industrial design is the process of determining the appearance of things that are used by industry. It is often divided into three different categories.

1. Product design: the look of the products themselves
2. Environmental design: the appearance of offices and factories
3. Information design: the design of computer networks, office information systems, and so on

Let's use for an example a calendar, which has elements of all three categories: It is a **PRODUCT**, and will be designed as such; it is also a piece of office furnishing; and it is a sort of information system. A calendar will have design elements to take account of all of these facets.

Design is the conscious effort to impose meaningful order.

Victor Papanek

DIARY PANEL

A diary panel consists of a number of shoppers who use diaries to keep a regular (daily, weekly, and so on) record of all their purchases of a number of selected products. The Market Research Corporation of America (MCA) empanels 7,500 families located throughout the United States to note all their food and drug purchases during a week. The analysis of their diaries is offered for sale. Other research companies collect other types of diaries — for example, of people's television viewing habits and fast-food eating behavior.

DIFFERENTIATED MARKETING

See MARKET SEGMENTATION

DIFFUSION

The process by which a new product is adopted by more and more consumers over time. At first, only individuals who are wholly confident about the new product or who love taking risks will buy it. Once these "innovators" have adopted the product, it will be tried by a larger group, known as "early adopters." They are the opinion leaders who will influence wider acceptance of the PRODUCT.

Diffusion can be speeded up by making ADOPTION seem less risky. Cosmetics manufacturers give samples away free or at a special introductory price; manufacturers install machines on a six-month trial basis; or (as in IBM's case) give away thousands of personal computers to business schools in order to secure rapid consumer acceptance beyond the circle of early adopters.

DIRECTIONAL POLICY MATRIX

A classification of products developed by the Shell Oil Company. It is based on two dimensions:

- The profitability of the market segment in which the business operates
- The competitive position of the business in that segment

A product's position on the matrix suggests its future; for example, the matrix's prognosis for a PRODUCT with an average competitive position in a MARKET that has a poor prospect of future profitability is of phased withdrawal from that market.

DIRECT MAIL

The sending of advertising and promotional material directly to consumers. Usually associated with mail order selling, direct mail has a much wider range of purposes, including appeals for money and political support. It is used by a wide range of organizations, from American Express to *Time* magazine to specialist retailers such as Banana Republic.

The great advantage of direct mail is that marketers can target their audiences with great precision. Life Style Selector, for example, a company based in Denver, has a DATABASE of 10 million names and addresses, each identified by demographic and consumption information. Such firms make it possible for marketers to select carefully the most likely buyers of virtually any product.

Although direct mail is sometimes disparagingly referred to as "JUNK MAIL," research suggests that less than one mailing in five goes into a wastebasket unread.

DIRECT MARKETING

The shortest channel of **DISTRIBUTION**: when a manufacturer of a **PRODUCT** deals directly with the consumer. Farmers who advertise "Potatoes for Sale" or "Pick Your Own Strawberries" at their gate are engaging in direct marketing. So are salespeople who call directly at people's homes selling such things as insurance, cosmetics, or encyclopedias.

MAIL ORDER accounts for the largest segment of direct marketing. Other forms include the following:

- Telephone selling
- Selling through newspaper advertisements
- **DIRECT MAIL**, driven increasingly from a computerized database

DIRECT RESPONSE ADVERTISING

The sort of advertisement that has a telephone number customers can call immediately to order the goods or services being advertised. Long popular in the printed media, direct response advertising is being used increasingly on television. Charities often give a telephone number for viewers to call as soon as the advertisement is off the air.

DISCRETIONARY INCOME

That part of a consumer's disposable income that is not spoken for in advance in the form of mortgage or consumer-credit repayments, school fees, or other standing orders and direct debits. Marketers are always looking for people with high levels of discretionary income. They are not the same as wealthy people; wealthy people may have high incomes that are almost all spoken for, particularly at certain stages in their lives.

Although **EMPTY NESTERS** expect their incomes to fall as they get older and retire, their discretionary income may actually rise as the expense of raising children and maintaining a large home gradually disappears.

DISPOSABLE INCOME

A slightly different economic concept from **DISCRETIONARY INCOME**. Disposable income is that income left to consumers after they have paid all compulsory levies from the government such as direct income taxes, property taxes, or social security taxes. Disposable income will always be greater than discretionary income.

DISTRIBUTION

A key marketing function: the process of getting products to consumers. Although some manufacturers can and do sell direct to consumers (see **DIRECT MARKETING**), practical considerations require most to use a distribution system composed of independent middlemen, usually wholesalers, retailers, or distributors.

These intermediaries carry out critically important marketing activities such as buying and selling, sorting and storing, transporting, and financing products as they move from producer to consumer, all of which are necessary functions if products are to be found by consumers in the right place at the right time and at the right price.

Distribution can also refer to a measure of market penetration: the number of retail outlets that stock and sell a particular product as a percentage of all outlets that could possibly sell that product.

DISTRIBUTION CHANNEL

The network of companies that moves goods from the manufacturer to the consumer.

DISTRIBUTOR

A **WHOLESALER** of industrial products. Distributors are the major force in industrial distribution channels. Distributors sell goods to manufacturers. They also provide warehousing and a range of other services such as delivery, credit, order processing, and technical advice.

As sellers to manufacturers, they need to be able to respond quickly to a customer's needs so that its production is not disrupted. As part of their ability to respond quickly, many distributors provide a repair service for the goods they sell, acting on behalf of the original manufacturer.

DMBB

See D'ARCY, MASIUS, BENTON & BOWLES

DMU

See DECISION-MAKING UNIT

DOWNSCALE MARKET

See UPSCALE MARKET

DRIP CAMPAIGN

An ADVERTISING CAMPAIGN in which the advertisements are shown infrequently over a long period of time.

DUMPING

Offering goods for sale in a foreign market at prices lower than those prevailing in their domestic market. Dumping amounts to prima facie evidence of unfair competition and is against the rules of the General Agreement on Tariffs and Trade (GATT). Proof that dumping has taken place is, however, often difficult to establish. Exchange-rate fluctuations and the use of transfer-pricing methods that might themselves be quite legitimate can blur the most genuine attempt to compare export prices with domestic prices.

EFFIE AWARDS

Annual awards presented by the New York chapter of the **AMERICAN MARKETING ASSOCIATION** to advertising agencies and their clients for the quality and effectiveness of advertisements in a number of different categories. Most nations have an equivalent form of annual advertising award. In Hong Kong they are called "Golden Junks"; in Turkey they are "Glass Apples."

ELASTICITY

An economic concept that relates the change in one variable to the change in another. A piece of elastic's elasticity is the extra distance it stretches for every extra unit of weight that is suspended from it. The elasticity of demand in a particular market is the change in sales that results from a unit increase or decrease in the product's price.

ELECTRONIC POINT OF SALE

Commonly known by the acronym **POS**. A checkout counter that is equipped with the necessary electronic gadgetry to read a **BAR CODE**. The codes are passed over an electronic scanner placed in the counter or are read by using a hand-held electronic light pen.

The information then passes into the store's computer, where it can be used to maintain up-to-the-minute stock control. The information can also be printed out as a fully itemized receipt for the customer.

POS is not to be confused with EFTPOS (electronic funds transfer at the **POINT OF SALE**). EFTPOS refers to the electronic technology that enables consumers to pay for goods with a plastic card, which debits their bank account directly and immediately. EFTPOS eliminates the time-consuming task of writing checks, but it gives the customer no period of credit at all.

EMPTY NESTERS

Families whose children have flown the nest and set up their own independent households. Such people form an interesting group of consumers for marketers. They have particularly high levels of DISCRETIONARY INCOME because their housing costs have been reduced (by paying off the mortgage or moving to a smaller home) and the cost of supporting their children has dropped dramatically. Empty nesters (particularly those in the 50–60 age group) are increasingly having their discretionary income further enhanced by inheritance from parents who are dying later and leaving ever larger capital sums.

EMULATOR

One of the categories in a well-known U.S. classification of consumers (see LIFESTYLE).

END-USER

The consumer who actually uses a PRODUCT. This may not be the same as the person who is responsible for making the decision to purchase that product, which is an important point for marketers to remember. For example, babies do not decide what baby food they are to be the end-users of; and many men do not decide what suits, socks, or shirts they are to be the end-users of.

I sell enthusiasm.

Silvio Berlusconi, Italian television magnate

ENVIRONMENTAL SCANNING

The systematic examination of the business environment with a view to identifying marketing opportunities and threats. The business environment includes competitors, the domestic economy, trade patterns, cultural and social trends, and technology. Nowadays it also includes attitudes to the environment itself. The powerful green consumer movement has provided many marketing threats; but it has thrown up many marketing opportunities as well.

ETHICAL GOODS

An advertising industry expression for drugs and equipment sold to the medical profession and not directly to the general public. There are some peculiar marketing features associated with such products.

- They are sold to a small group of knowledgeable consumers, each of which can be responsible (through prescriptions) for a large amount of consumption.
- They are often produced by drug companies under PATENT, so they have no direct competition.

It takes up to 40 dumb animals to make a fur coat, but only one to wear it.

Antifur campaign

EXCLUSIVE DISTRIBUTION

The right given by a manufacturer to a RETAILER to be the sole vendor of the manufacturer's products in a given geographical area (a territory), similar in many ways to certain sorts of franchising. Business computers, high-quality luggage, and fine china are some of the products typically sold on an exclusive distribution basis.

The system gives manufacturers greater control over their distribution networks, especially with regard to their products' retail prices and the services that are offered with them.

EXHIBITION

Using large exhibition halls (often of more than 1,000,000 square feet) for manufacturers in the same industry to test out their new products and to meet customers is a well-established practice. The commonest reason cited for attending exhibitions is the "need to keep abreast of technology." The exhibitions industry even has its own exhibition. Called International Confex, it was held in London in 1992.

EXPECTATIONS

A word that economists have adopted to refer to people's beliefs about the economic future. To some extent these are self-fulfilling. If business people expect the future to be rosy, they will invest more; the future is then indeed more likely to be rosy.

Expectations also play a great part in the business of MARKETING. To advertise a new product as something that it is not is more damaging than not to advertise it at all. If consumers' expectations are frustrated after they have purchased a PRODUCT, not only will they not buy it again but they will also feel badly done by. They may then spread unfavorable WORD-OF-MOUTH ADVERTISING.

Experts should be always on tap, but never on top.

Anon

EXTENDED GUARANTEE

A guarantee that a manufacturer or RETAILER offers (at a price) to a customer for a specified period of time beyond the term of the original guarantee. It is a prolonged insurance policy against breakdown.

The name Exxon was the result of a search for a word that was meaningless and without connotation in any language. Ten thousand names were produced by a computer. These were reduced to 234 by extensive opinion polls among 7,000 people, and thence to six. These six were then carefully examined for meaninglessness in more than 100 languages.

FACT BOOK

A file of information about a product's history. Typically it contains the following:

- Data on the product's sales, DISTRIBUTION, and competition
- A profile of the product's customers
- Any relevant marketing research findings
- A detailed record of the product's performance over time in relation to the marketing effort made on its behalf

Fact books are retained by company brand managers and by advertising agency account managers.

FAD

A product that is suddenly and briefly taken up with great enthusiasm, characterized by rapid sales growth and almost equally rapid sales decline. Recent fads include Rubik's cube, the skateboard, the filofax, and platform shoes.

FAMILY LIFE CYCLE

A description of the six ages of the family based on age, marital status, and presence or absence of children. The cycle has proved useful in defining the demand for certain goods and services because each stage produces distinguishable needs and interests. The six stages of the cycle are as follows:

1. Young single people
2. Young couples with no children
3. Young couples whose youngest child is under six
4. Couples with dependent children
5. Older couples with no children at home
6. Older single people

FASHION GOODS

Goods where style and design are all-important. Best illustrated by women's clothing, where what starts off in haute couture salons of Paris and Milan is imitated by mass manufacturers and then appears briefly in main-street shops before disappearing to make way for the next wave of fashion goods to have been copied from the runway. Marketing goods with such a short shelf life requires special skills.

FAST FOOD

The production of limited and standardized menus for customers to eat on the premises or to take away. Fast-food outlets have four particular characteristics.

1. The premises are bright, basic, and clean.
2. Staff members are trained to be cheerful and helpful.
3. Quality of food is consistent.
4. Outlets are often franchised.

Fast food was the fastest-growing retailing innovation in recent decades. Although hamburger joints and pizza parlors existed before 1952, there was no really fast food until McDonald's raised its golden arches for the first time that year. Its pioneering formula for hamburgers has been followed by formulas for pizza, chicken pieces, tacos, doughnuts, croissants, and even fish 'n chips, as at the Long John Silver's chain in the United States.

FAST-MOVING CONSUMER GOODS

The kinds of products that are usually sold in supermarkets and that move off the shelves quickly such as toothpaste and chewing gum. Fast-moving consumer goods (FMCGs) require in-store stocks of them to be constantly replenished.

Fiat was founded in 1899 as Fabbrica Italiana Automobili Torino, the Italian automobile company of Turin.

FIELD RESEARCH

MARKETING RESEARCH carried out in the "field" through interviews, GROUP DISCUSSION, and so on, as opposed to SECONDARY RESEARCH. In practice, field research is more likely to be carried out by telephone.

FLANKER BRAND

A new brand introduced by a company that already markets a BRAND in the same product category. For example, a diet mayonnaise by Hellmann's. (See also LINE EXTENSION)

FLASH PACK

A package on which a sales promotion message (usually a price reduction) is printed prominently. Products in flash packs are offered in limited quantities and/or for limited periods of time.

FOCUS GROUP

A type of MARKETING RESEARCH where groups of people are gathered together for an informal discussion for the purposes of learning more about attitudes and buying behaviors for a PRODUCT. The interviewer/chairperson has an agenda of topics to cover, but questionnaires are not used.

Interaction within the group is designed to encourage wide-ranging exploration of a subject. Focus groups are typically used in NEW PRODUCT DEVELOPMENT in order to test ideas and products. They are also used for QUALITATIVE RESEARCH on existing products and sometimes by advertising agencies to try out new bits of copy.

*Almost everybody knows that Ford is the name
of Henry Ford, the man who founded the company. But how many realize that Chevrolet,
Chrysler, Citröen, and Porsche are also the
names of men who were closely involved with
the development of the cars named after them?*

FRANCHISE

A contractual agreement in which one party (the franchisor)
sells the right to market goods or services to another party (the
franchisee). McDonald's and Kentucky Fried Chicken are long-
standing examples of successful retail franchises that started in
the United States. Examples that started in Europe (and outside
the fast-food business) are Benetton and The Body Shop.

Franchising can also take place at the wholesale level. Both
Coca-Cola and Pepsi-Cola built up their worldwide businesses
by franchising their secret ingredients to wholesale bottlers who
then produced and bottled the beverages and distributed them
to retailers.

In retail franchising the franchisor provides the franchisee
with a large number of marketing services. In return, the franchisee purchases equipment and supplies, pays franchising fees
(often a large initial fee), and frequently remits a percentage of
revenues.

The franchisee is usually given exclusive selling rights in a
particular area, although not by Benetton, which has successfully defended its right (in both Italy and the United States) to
grant a franchise to shops on opposite sides of the same street.

FREQUENCY DISTRIBUTION

A common way of presenting marketing research statistics, according to the frequency with which particular responses are
given. For example, suppose a researcher is asking people for
their response to an advertisement that they have just seen.

They may be offered several choices of response: very favorable, favorable, indifferent, hostile, or very hostile.

The researcher's findings can then be plotted as a chart, with the number of respondents on one axis and the type of response on the other. Such a chart, showing the frequency distribution, will give a clearer picture of the overall response to the advertisement.

FULFILLMENT

The process of fulfilling orders received through direct mail selling. In the case of a magazine subscription, for example, fulfillment will involve the following:

- Sending magazines to the subscriber for the period of time paid for
- Sending reminders as and when the subscription needs to be renewed
- Leaving a trail so that any problems with a particular subscriber can be followed up

Most such fulfillment systems nowadays are computer based. (See KEY CODE)

FUNCTIONALISM

An approach to the study of MARKETING that focuses on the functions of marketing rather than its institutions. Functionalism is particularly associated with Wroe Anderson and Ed McGarry. McGarry defined the following functions of marketing:

- Contactual: searching out buyers and sellers
- MERCHANDISING: fitting the goods to market requirements
- PRICING: selecting a price high enough to make production possible and low enough to induce users to accept the goods
- Propaganda: conditioning buyers or sellers to a favorable attitude toward the PRODUCT or its sponsor
- Physical distribution: transporting and storing the goods

GAP ANALYSIS

A procedure for discovering marketing opportunities represented by gaps in a market. There are three important areas in which to look for gaps:

1. A neglected consumer group
2. A deficiency in existing product offerings
3. A sector suitable for exploitation because of some new technological development

Marketing researchers have developed sophisticated techniques for conducting gap analysis. (See **PERCEPTUAL MAPPING**)

GENERAL ELECTRIC BUSINESS SCREEN

A method for **PORTFOLIO ANALYSIS** that overcomes some of the limitations of the growth/share matrix. The analysis was developed jointly by McKinsey and General Electric.

The screen is more complex than in the growth/share matrix, having nine rather than four cells. It also considers more subtle variables such as ease of competitive entry, production efficiency, market attractiveness, and investment alternatives.

GENERIC BRANDS

Goods that are sold with no **ADVERTISING** or **PROMOTION**, and usually in plain, undecorated **PACKAGING**. Often referred to as Brand-X goods, generics represent a response to criticism that too much money is spent on **MARKETING**, and that no-frills products allow substantial price reductions. Generics have made strong inroads into commodity-type grocery products like soap and bathroom tissue. The key here is that the **PRODUCT** does not have a brand name. The package just says "Beer" or "Detergent," and so forth.

Generics can refer to goods that are nonproprietary, in particular to drugs and pharmaceuticals that have come off PATENT. Generic drugs can be manufactured and sold by anybody.

GENERIC NAME

The name of a class or category of products: "computers," for example, or "soups." Sometimes the name of a successful brand comes to be used as a generic name. Formica, elastic, and cellophane are three former brand names that have become generic.

GEO-DEMOGRAPHICS

A system of categorizing residential areas into different neighborhood types. Geo-demographics is widely believed to provide a better basis for predicting consumer behavior than alternative methods such as classifying a HOUSEHOLD according to the occupation of the main breadwinner, for example. It has been widely used by banks and retailers to determine where to locate new outlets and by marketing researchers in locating particular samples for their questionnaires.

GLOBAL BRAND

A PRODUCT that has a brand name which is universally recognized; for example, Coca-Cola, McDonald's, IBM, Levi, and Hilton. Some marketers speculate that the world will shortly be dominated by global brands because of the productive and marketing capability of large multinational companies. Some shoppers suspect that it already is.

The idea of global brands gained respectability through a famous article in the *Harvard Business Review* (HBR) of May–June 1983. Called "The Globalization of Markets," it was written by Theodore Levitt, a professor of MARKETING at Harvard who subsequently became editor of the HBR. The article opened with this assertion:

> *A powerful force now drives the world toward a single converging commonality, and that force is technology . . . the*

*result is a new commercial reality — the emergence of
global markets for standardized consumer products on a
previously unimagined scale of magnitude. Corporations
geared to this new reality benefit from enormous economies of scale in production, distribution, marketing, and
management.*

The marketing of global products makes assumptions about
the universality of human needs and wants, but marketers rec-
ognize that global brands cannot be marketed in the same way
in every country. Procter & Gamble markets its Pampers disposable diapers in more than 70 countries, but in each country the
MARKETING MIX is tailored to the requirements of the **MARKET**
in terms of price, **DISTRIBUTION**, and **ADVERTISING**.

Brand names sometimes encounter unexpected difficulties
when crossing international borders. For example, Ireland's Irish
Mist liqueur came up against unexpected problems in selling to
German-speaking markets; in German "mist" means "manure." Likewise the United Kingdom's Cadbury Schweppes declined to buy a French soft drink that was offered to it. The
drink was called Pschitt. Timotei shampoo is one of the few
new products over the past 20 years that has successfully gone
global. It started life in Finland as a small deodorant brand
within the Unilever empire. In Finnish its name means "grass,"
but there the product wilted. Unilever's Swedish company spot-
ted its potential as a pure and mild shampoo in an environmentally conscious age; and it has not looked back.

*Goodyear and Firestone, which now sound such
suitable names for tire companies that we can
only imagine they were specially created for the
purpose, are in fact the names of the men who
set up the companies.*

GLOBAL MARKETING

Companies are increasingly selling their products outside their domestic market. Some foreign brands have become so familiar that consumers assume they are manufactured by indigenous companies. For example, who knows that Nescafé is made by a Swiss company, Baskin and Robbins ice cream by a British company, and Crest toothpaste by a U.S. company?

The importance of global markets to U.S. firms cannot be overstated. Coca-Cola, for example, derives two-thirds of its sales and three-fourths of its profits from outside the United States. Today, even small firms can enter global markets through exports and joint venture partnerships.

GREY

One of the ten biggest advertising agency groups in the world. A long-established firm with a reputation for conservative financial management and stable relationships with its clients. Despite its conservative bent, it has grown fast in Europe in recent years.

GROUP DISCUSSION

Synonymous with FOCUS GROUP.

Habit buying

When a consumer repeatedly buys the same brand. Habit buying is believed to imply the absence of dissatisfaction with a **BRAND** rather than any positive loyalty to it. It is usually associated with the purchase of a **LOW-INVOLVEMENT PRODUCT** and can often be broken by an attractive sales promotion.

Hakuhodo

Japan's oldest and second-largest **ADVERTISING AGENCY**. It has not yet spread its wings far outside Japan, but it opened a New York office in 1960 and formed a partnership with **LINTAS**.

It also has a tie with Daniel J. Edelman, a large U.S. public relations firm.

---

*We're not in the hamburger business;
we're in show business.*

Ray Kroc, founder of McDonald's

Hard sell

Anything that is deemed to be aggressive selling.

Harvesting strategy

The reaping of short-term profit from a **PRODUCT** prior to withdrawing it from the **MARKET**. If it has been decided that a product is coming to the end of its **PRODUCT LIFE CYCLE**, marketing expenditure on it will be reduced; typically, **ADVERTISING** will be withdrawn. Because the effects of earlier advertising will still be felt, the product will continue to sell, ideally producing attractive net profits during its last days.

Some products' last days can spread into years if large enough bands of die-hard customers exist. Ipana toothpaste and Life-buoy soap both lived on profitably years after their marketing support had been withdrawn.

HEAVY USER

That segment of a MARKET that accounts for the bulk of its sales. Not all markets have a pronounced concentration on a few buyers, but where such heavy users exist there is little point in directing marketing effort at other groups. Heineken has said that it would use direct mail to advertise its lager to the 9% of men who drink 65% of it, if only there were a way of finding out their names and addresses. Marketers refer to the 20/80 rule: For many products the top 20% of customers — defined as heavy users — often account for up to 80% of sales.

HIERARCHY OF EFFECTS

The steps in the process of persuading somebody to buy something. The hierarchy moves through the following stages:

- Awareness
- Knowledge
- Liking
- Preference
- Conviction
- Purchase

Marketing communications are constructed with this hierarchy in mind; and salespeople will often follow these steps in making a sales presentation. (See also AIDA)

HIGH-INVOLVEMENT PRODUCT

A PRODUCT over which consumers take time and trouble to reach a purchasing decision; goods for which they shop around, comparing prices or financing arrangements.

Consumers take this sort of trouble over their purchases when there are elements of self-image, cost, or product performance involved. Cars, homes, customized kitchens, electronics, and package tours are some examples of high-involvement products.

Home audit

MARKETING RESEARCH conducted in the home by using a **DIARY PANEL** to record on a regular basis (weekly or monthly) what products householders buy, and how often they buy them.

The Hoover vacuum cleaner was first manufactured and marketed by a company owned by William Henry Hoover. But it was actually invented by one J. Murray Spangler, a caretaker from Ohio. We could have easily been cleaning our carpets nowadays with a Spangler.

Household

The people who live together and who constitute the fundamental unit in much **MARKETING RESEARCH**. Households are of particular interest because most consumption is done by household units rather than by individuals. The purchase of many consumer durables, like vacuum cleaners, dishwashers, or videocassette recorders, is more closely related to the number of households in a population (each of which can contain a number of people) than it is to the number of individuals.

Hypermarket

Anglicization of *hypermarché*, a French invention. The hypermarket is a store that is bigger than a **SUPERMARKET** and sells a wider range of products than the fast-moving consumer goods that people expect to find in a supermarket. The key is to provide consumers with "one-stop shopping" for all their needs.

IMAGE

The picture, feeling, or association that the name of a BRAND conjures up in a person's mind. A product's image is what that PRODUCT means to a person. For example, Volvo cars mean safety; Jaguar cars mean class.

Nations also have images and those images can change over time: "Made in Japan" used to mean cheap and shoddy; now it means high quality, high tech, and higher prices.

An ounce of image is worth a pound of performance.

Lawrence Peter

IMPULSE BUYING

Spur-of-the moment decisions to buy, made at the time of purchase. Goods that are apt to be bought impulsively (magazines, candy bars, chewing gum) are usually placed close to the POINT OF SALE. Goods that are bought routinely — cereals or shampoo, for example — may also be subject to impulse buying.

If every new product is stamped "improved," then what were we buying before?

Anon

INCENTIVE MARKETING

An umbrella term for all the special techniques used to persuade consumers to buy products; for example, SAMPLING, PREMIUM

OFFER, COUPON, SELF-LIQUIDATING OFFER. More commonly called sales promotion.

INDUSTRIAL ADVERTISING

See BUSINESS-TO-BUSINESS ADVERTISING

INDUSTRIAL GOODS

Goods that are purchased mainly for use in the production of other goods, in contrast to consumer goods. They include such things as machines, tools, components, and lubricants. Few goods are exclusively industrial; for example, lubricants are also sold directly to consumers.

INERTIA SELLING

A form of selling familiar to anyone who has ever belonged to a book club. If you do not cancel the monthly selection, then you receive the book. The sale is made as a result of inertia — that is, the customer's failure to take any action to stop it.

INNOVATION

The process of developing and introducing a new product or new product design to the MARKET. Under pressure of competition, companies try to preserve their competitive advantage by continuous product innovation. As the rate of innovation increases, the time that a PRODUCT has in which to produce a profit for the company is reduced. That puts more pressure on the company to innovate, and so the spiral of innovation continues.

The successful management of the process of innovation is crucial to most companies' success. Some concentrate their efforts on bringing out products based on established market demand — a new detergent, for example, or a new line of cosmetics. Other companies are true innovators, developing technological firsts such as the home computer or the compact disc player.

3M insists that at least 25% of its sales come from products that did not exist five years earlier. This is one way to check that the process of innovation is continuing at a satisfactory pace.

INNOVATORS

Consumers who are the first to try new products, typically only a small percentage of the population. Research suggests that innovators tend to be well educated, well informed, well to do, open minded, upwardly mobile, and reachable by the mass media. They are also only a small percentage of the total population compared with other identified consumer types.

	%
Innovators	2.5
Early adopters	13.5
Early majority	34.0
Late majority	34.0
Laggards	16.0

The same people will not be innovators for every product. A new method of seed drilling will appeal to one group of innovators, while digital audio tape will appeal to another. Marketers always try to identify the innovator group for any given product, and concentrate their initial efforts on them.

INSTALLMENT CREDIT

An arrangement between a buyer and a seller whereby the buyer pays for goods or services in installments over time; the vendor thus effectively extends credit to the buyer, even though there may be no formal payment of interest involved.

INSTITUTIONAL ADVERTISING

Most advertising is concerned with goods and services, but there are many organizations that simply advertise themselves. Companies that market brands conspicuously linked with the company name (DuPont, for example) anticipate that favorable public reaction to their corporate advertising will spill over to their products.

Companies that may create public hostility through their operations — mining, oil, chemical, or nuclear power companies, for example — use institutional advertising to try to counteract negative reactions. Chevron Oil, for example, advertised the fact that it was preserving the habitat of a tiny endangered species of butterfly in the middle of its giant refinery and right next to the huge Los Angeles international airport.

In the United Kingdom Shell Oil put out an advertisement showing a picture of a beautiful Welsh valley. The company asked viewers what they would do to protect the valley against the ravages of a bulldozer carving out a way for a pipeline. Shell went on to reveal that it had already laid a pipeline in the valley and had restored it to the condition in which viewers were seeing it.

Giant multinational conglomerates with portfolios that include a wide range of businesses also use institutional advertising to establish their names. United Technologies ran a series of newspaper ads that featured homilies on profound but non-controversial subjects. Only the name of the company appeared at the bottom of the page; there was no mention of any product. The series proved very popular, eliciting thousands of requests for reprints.

INTEGRATED COMMUNICATIONS

Increasingly popular with marketing directors, this phrase refers to the coordination of all aspects of product promotion, from ADVERTISING to DIRECT MAIL. (See also ABOVE-THE-LINE)

INTENTIONS

Attempts are sometimes made to forecast sales on the basis of consumers' stated intentions to buy. Research is undertaken, particularly in the field of INDUSTRIAL GOODS, to ascertain such intentions. However, since the respondent has little to lose by his or her answers, such research is not always a very sound basis for sales forecasting.

INTERACTIVE MARKETING

An approach to MARKETING that stresses that both buyers and sellers are active in decision making, particularly in industrial markets. Standard models of marketing have been criticized for being too deterministic, suggesting that suppliers have total control over the marketing process and that customers are passive.

Interactive marketing stresses that marketing success is dependent on the competence and ability of the individuals and organizations involved in the process of interaction. It maintains that an understanding of the relationship and interdependence between supplier and customer is essential to good marketing. Important aspects of the interaction are the following:

- The atmosphere surrounding the relationship
- The degree of cooperation and conflict
- The overall social distance between buyers and sellers

INTERPUBLIC

A large U.S. holding company that owns two big international advertising agencies, MCCANN ERICKSON and LINTAS, and several smaller ones as well.

Having several agencies within one group allows the company to work for more than one firm in each industrial sector. Otherwise, in order to avoid conflicts of interest, no single agency would work for example, for both Coca-Cola and PepsiCo.

Interpublic has also been a pioneer in the production of television material around which to wrap advertisements, and in having a marketing research firm and a sales promotion firm under the corporate umbrella.

JINGLE

A catchy little tune that can become a powerful marketing tool when played as part of a television commercial.

Jingles used to be written and commissioned especially for particular advertisements, and a very small number of them would subsequently become popular hit songs. In recent years, however, advertisers have increasingly used snippets of popular old songs as jingles. In particular, they have used songs which evoke nostalgia among **BABY BOOMERS** — today's big spenders — for the years of their youth, the 1960s. The trend was led by Levi Strauss, which has often (and very successfully) put nostalgia at the center of its advertising message.

If you've got nothing to say, sing it.

Advertising industry advice

JUDGMENT SAMPLING

The selection of respondents for a survey on the basis of criteria judged by the researcher to be the most appropriate for the purposes of the research.

Judgment sampling is most frequently used in industrial marketing research. In an industry dominated by a few manufacturers, the researcher may decide that a sample representative of those few is more significant than one that attempts to embrace all manufacturers in the industry.

JUNK MAIL

Promotional and advertising material of all kinds that arrives unsolicited in the daily mail. The judgment that the term implies is picturesque, but not entirely accurate. (See **DIRECT MAIL**)

KEY CODE

The alphanumeric code that marketers put on their direct mail order blanks (usually near the address) so they can analyze the response to **DIRECT MAIL**. Key coding enables them to find out such things as:

- Which list a respondent came from
- What type of offer was made to him or her
- What social category the respondent belongs to

Kleenex, a word that has almost became a generic brand name — Kimberly-Clark spends millions of dollars each year to prevent it from becoming generic — was invented in the 1920s, one of a spate of contemporary no-meaning names that ended in "x." The spate included Lux, Pyrex, and Cutex.

KNOCKING COPY

Copy that is critical of a competitor's product. (See **COMPARATIVE ADVERTISING**)

Kodak, generally agreed to be one of the most successful brand names ever (having two essential ingredients: alliteration and the "k" sound), was chosen by George Eastman in 1888. Eastman once explained how the name came to him: "I knew a trade name must be short, vigorous, incapable of being misspelled to an extent that it will destroy its identity, and in order to satisfy

*trademark laws it must mean nothing. The letter
'k' had been a favorite with me; it seemed a
strong, incisive sort of letter."*

Philip Kotler

One of the most famous American marketing gurus and author
of the classic standard textbook *Marketing Management.*

Kotler has been something of a counterweight to the Theodore Levitt school of global marketing, arguing that markets are
becoming more fragmented, not less. For instance, he has made
the following commentary.

*The heart of modern strategic marketing can be described
as STP marketing, namely segmenting, targeting and positioning. This does not obviate the importance of LGD marketing — lunch, golf, and dinner marketing — but rather
provides the broader framework for strategic success in the
marketplace. Today's companies are finding it increasingly
unrewarding to practice mass marketing or product variety
marketing. Mass markets are becoming "demassified."
They are dissolving into hundreds of micromarkets.*

LAUNCH

The introduction of a new product on to the **MARKET**. This can be done in two ways: either with a whimper or with a bang.

The whimper approach is to dribble the product on to a small part of the whole market in a sort of **TEST MARKETING** or to launch it nationally without any **ADVERTISING** in the hope that word-of-mouth will make it succeed. The latter approach worked with the popular game Trivial Pursuit, for example, but has failed in many other instances.

Most big companies use a "roll out" strategy with a big bang in a small geographic area and then roll out to other markets as capacity allows.

Either lead, follow or get out of my way.

Sign on the desk of Ted Turner, founder of CNN

LEASED DEPARTMENT

A small space in a **DEPARTMENT STORE**, hotel, or office building from which a **RETAILER** is given the right to sell his or her specialized products or services. With the re-emergence of leased departments, department stores have begun to resemble small shopping malls.

LEASING

A contractual arrangement in which the use of a piece of equipment over a period of time is sold by one party (the lessor) to another party (the lessee).

Leasing rather than outright purchase is preferred by many companies because it reduces the demand on cash flow in the short term (there is little or no capital outlay), and it may guarantee service from the lessee (important in the case of complicated equipment). It also offers the prospect of updating products on favorable terms. Firms leasing computers or company cars, for example, have exploited this marketing opportunity.

Licensing

Selling the right to use some process, **TRADEMARK**, **PATENT**, or the like in return for a fee or for the payment of royalties. Licensing is a relatively low-risk way of entering a foreign market: the licensee (the purchaser of the right) bears most of the risks incurred. If the licensee is an effective marketer, the licenser (the seller of the right) can reap a rich reward for little risk.

Licensing is often used to enter markets where direct entry is difficult; for example, in Japan or Eastern Europe. Corning Glass licensed the right to manufacture television tubes to a then-Yugoslav state corporation; Massey-Ferguson gave a Polish company the right to manufacture its branded tractors.

Lifestyle

The way people choose to live, based on their attitude toward life. Segmenting markets according to lifestyle is popular among researchers trying to classify groups of consumers in ways that relate to their behavior in stores.

One such classification, developed by the Stanford Research Institute, is called **VALUES AND LIFESTYLES** (VALS). It contains the following.

- Belongers: patriotic, stable, sentimental traditionalists who are content with their lives
- Achievers: prosperous, self-assured, middle-aged materialists
- Emulators: ambitious young adults trying to break into the system
- I-am-me group: impulsive, experimental, a bit narcissistic

- Societally conscious: mature, successful, mission-oriented people who like causes
- Survivors: the old and poor, with little optimism about the future
- Sustainers: resentful of their condition in trying to make ends meet

Most consumers probably feel that they fall into several different VALS categories in their lifetimes.

LINE EXTENSION

Increasing a **PRODUCT LINE** by adding variations of an existing brand. When a company has a successful brand, there is a temptation to use the brand name on other products. Thus a well-known brand of hand lotion might have variants for dry skin, sensitive skin, detergent-damaged skin, and so on.

Line extension runs the risk of weakening the brand name. If the lotion for sensitive skin is no good, then the original lotion's image suffers. It also runs the risk of consumers substituting the new product for an old one.

LINE FILLING

Adding more products to an existing **PRODUCT LINE** in order to leave no gaps for competitors to move into. Procter & Gamble, a past master at line filling, has 24 brands of laundry detergent (from Bold to Tide). Each is differentiated in some way from the others.

When product lines are increased by moving **UPMARKET** or **DOWNMARKET** to attract new customers, the process is sometimes called line stretching. In the market for office photocopiers the major manufacturers have stretched the line both upward (to large, high-speed multifunctional machines with sophisticated sorting capacity) and downward to small machines that are low enough in price to be purchased for the home.

LINTAS

A large **ADVERTISING AGENCY** owned by the **INTERPUBLIC GROUP**.

LIST BROKER

An organization that gathers lists of names and addresses and sells them to marketers for direct marketing purposes. To some extent the broker can tailor lists according to the marketer's needs; for example, children under 15 living in households above a certain income level might be worth mailing for the launch of a new brand of expensive ice cream. In the United States alone there are as many as 10,000 different lists available.

A secondary industry is that of using so-called de-duplication computer programs to eliminate the duplication of names and addresses from a number of lists. The computer matches names and addresses on one disc with those on another, but it cannot cope with slight differences in postal codes or in the spelling of street names.

So duplication is still not uncommon in **DIRECT MAIL**.

Exports are becoming obsolete, because they are too slow. Marketers today must sell the latest product everywhere at once, and that means producing locally.

Carlo De Benedetti, Olivetti

LOCALIZATION

Originally this referred to the tendency of industries to stick together: jewelers in one district, lacemakers in another, hosiers in yet another.

In modern parlance localization has come to have a very specific marketing meaning, the exact opposite of globalization: the tailoring of goods and services for small local markets, fully taking into account a market's geographical and cultural differences.

The debate between those marketers in favor of globalization and those in favor of localization has not been resolved other than by the creation of the slogan: "Think global, act local." But Procter & Gamble, which once believed that its great marketing prowess could brush aside all cultural differences, has now acknowledged that it must account for local differences and fine-tune its "world products" accordingly.

Lego, the educational toy, is not Latin for "I read," but Danish for "play well" (leg godt). Its inventor was a Danish carpenter called Ole Kirk Christiansen.

Loss leader

A retailing device whereby a particular product is priced at a loss in order to "lead" customers into the store. Once in the store it is hoped that they will buy not only the loss leader but also items on which the RETAILER makes a profit. Loss leaders are often sold on a limited availability basis "while stocks last" or "to the first 50 customers only."

Loss-leader pricing is a device to promote the retail outlet and not the product, so there are plenty of manufacturers who do not want their products to be used as loss leaders. Martini & Rossi, for example, has withheld supplies of its products from stores that have used them as loss leaders.

Low-involvement product

A PRODUCT purchased without much deliberation or forethought that involves neither ego nor much money; in other words, where a poor purchasing decision does not have very significant consequences.

The challenge for marketers is to try and make low-involvement products more interesting to consumers. Heavy advertising to develop **BRAND LOYALTY** is one device; for example, the old Lux soap ads that used to feature film stars' endorsements. While soap is not something that consumers want to become involved with, film stars are. Today, marketers turn to pop stars (Elton John, Michael Jackson, and Paula Abdul, for example) and professional athletes (Michael Jordan and Bo Jackson) to attract attention to their products.

MACRO MARKETING

A term taken from economics that refers to marketing when studied in the context of large aggregations rather than of small units. Macro marketing is concerned with the flow of goods and services from producers to consumers within whole economic systems and with the processes that direct such flows.

Micro marketing is concerned with marketing processes in individual companies and with consumers' and organizations' buying behavior.

MADISON AVENUE

A main north–south street in New York City that used to be home to the head offices of all the world's biggest advertising agencies. Madison Avenue became synonymous with the advertising industry as Wall Street did with banking and finance.

However, the industry has spread its wings in recent years. Not only are some of the biggest agencies now based in cities outside the United States, but some big U.S. agencies have their major offices outside New York in places like Chicago and Los Angeles.

MAIL ORDER

The use of the mail as a DISTRIBUTION CHANNEL to link the manufacturer, WHOLESALER and/or RETAILER directly with the consumer. Based on catalogue selling, L.L. Bean has a long-established mail order business.

Mail order used to be considered a downmarket way of selling, but the growth of operations such as the Banana Republic and Neiman-Marcus has shown that it can be made to appeal to more upmarket consumers as well.

Many credit card companies also run mail order businesses, sending little catalogues along with their bills and statements.

Their marketing logic for this is that since they have to pay to send enormous amounts of mail in any case, they might as well put something else in the envelopes. Their customer databases allow them to target effectively, increasing response to a very profitable level.

MANUFACTURER BRAND

A brand that is owned by the manufacturer (as opposed to a private-label brand, which is owned by a distributor).

Shakespeare was wrong. A rose by any other name would not smell as sweet . . . which is why the single most important decision in the marketing of perfume is the name.

Al Ries and Jack Trout

MARKET

In marketing terms, a group of consumers who share a particular characteristic that affects their needs or wants, and that makes them potential buyers of a PRODUCT. To be a market, a group must have all of these attributes:

- an interest in the product
- the resources to buy the product
- a willingness to spend money on the product

MARKETING

Officially defined by the AMERICAN MARKETING ASSOCIATION as "the process of planning and executing the conception, pricing, PROMOTION, and DISTRIBUTION of ideas, goods, and services to create exchanges that satisfy individual and organizational objectives." This definition applies to nonprofit organizations as well.

In *The Basic Arts of Marketing*, Prabhu Guptara identifies six activities that come under the umbrella title "marketing":

1. Identifying the needs of existing and potential customers (An emphasis on satisfying customer requirements is central to any definition of marketing.)
2. Determining the best product strategy
3. Ensuring the effective distribution of products
4. Informing customers of the existence of products and persuading them to buy those products
5. Determining the prices at which products should be sold
6. Ensuring that **AFTER-SALES SERVICE** is of the right quality

---

Marketing is everything, and everything is marketing.

Regis McKenna

Not everything that goes by the name "marketing" deserves it. It has become too fashionable. A grave-digger remains a grave-digger even when called a mortician; only the cost of the burial goes up.

Peter Drucker

MARKETING DEPARTMENT

The department in a company that is responsible for marketing; to some extent its size and form will depend on the size and nature of the company (whether it is in consumer goods or **INDUSTRIAL GOODS**, and so on).

In a typical company the head of marketing will be responsible for various functions:

- **ADVERTISING** and sales promotion
- Sales
- **MARKETING RESEARCH**
- Product planning
- Administration
- Product R&D/**NEW PRODUCT DEVELOPMENT**
- (Sometimes) **PUBLIC RELATIONS**

MARKETING FLOP

About 80% of all new products never become commercial successes. An enterprising Scot, Robert McMath, opened a "product museum" in Naples, New York, where some of these failures have been saved from total oblivion. Most of them represent pain and disappointment to some unknown small entrepreneur. But the mighty make mistakes too, and their failures often become more famous. Ford offered its large and powerful Edsel to a market that wanted smaller economic cars.

MARKETING MANAGEMENT

One of the four principal management functions in a company along with production management, financial management, and R&D.

There are ten identified responsibilities of marketing management:

1. Finding out the facts (**MARKETING RESEARCH**).
2. Making predictions from research (forecasting).
3. Designing products based on that research (**NEW PRODUCT DEVELOPMENT**).
4. Making sure they are products that customers want to buy (**BRAND MANAGEMENT**).

5. Deciding on quantities (budgeting).

6. Deciding at what price goods should be sold and for what profit (pricing policy).

7. Moving goods from their point of manufacture to their point of consumption (**DISTRIBUTION**).

8. Selling (sales management).

9. Persuading through communication (**ADVERTISING, PUBLIC RELATIONS**, and sales promotion).

10. **POSITIONING** and **PACKAGING** the product (product strategy, branding)

MARKETING MIX

A description of the various elements of the marketing process that must be coordinated to make up the total marketing effort. These elements are often summarized as the Four Ps.

1. **PRODUCT:** What product is going to be offered to the customer? What are its characteristics, its brand name, its **PACKAGING**? What additions can be made to the **PRODUCT LINE**?

2. Price: How much is the customer going to pay for the product? How are price levels to be adjusted in the light of consumers' responses and of competitors' behavior?

3. Place: How is the product going to get to where the customer is when the customer wants it? What type of wholesale and retail outlets are to be used? What is to be the geographical coverage?

4. **PROMOTION:** How is the customer going to know about the product and be persuaded to buy it? What **ADVERTISING** is to be used and what will be its nature, content, frequency, and reach? How much sales promotion and **PUBLICITY** are there to be? What sales force is needed and what will be its size, territories, and style of selling?

To reflect many companies' growing customer orientation, there is a tendency to refer less to the four Ps, and more to the Four Cs.

1. Customer value (from the buyer's point of view). This replaces product.

2. Cost to the customer. This is more than the price charged because it includes the cost of the customer's time and energy; it replaces price.

3. Convenience for the buyer. This replaces place.

4. Communication. This is a dialogue that replaces promotion (a monologue by the seller).

MARKETING PLAN

The plan drawn up by managers of products, brands, or markets to define their objectives and strategies. Typically, a marketing plan will consist of the following sections.

- An analysis of past marketing performance, with data on the relevant market (size, growth, consumer behavior, trends), the PRODUCT (sales, prices, profits), the competition (size, MARKET SHARE, strategies), DISTRIBUTION and the environment (demographic, economic, social, political, and technological trends). This leads to a statement on the company's strengths and weaknesses and the opportunities and threats facing it.

- The formulation of marketing objectives, in relation to financial objectives (profits, sales revenues, return on capital, and so on). The marketing objectives might be to increase the market share of the PRODUCT LINE by 3% over the planning period, or to increase the sales revenue of the BRAND by 5%. Whenever possible, marketing objectives are stated quantitatively, with a given time period for their achievement.

- The development of marketing strategies. For each objective, managers have to decide which of many possible strategies to follow. If the aim is to increase the product line's market share, a brand might be selected for increased marketing support, or another brand might be added to the line. The brand's sales revenues might be increased by using a special sales promotion. Or the price of the brand might be raised.
- The preparation of plans setting out what is to be done, who will do it, when, and at what cost.

MARKETING RESEARCH

The collection and analysis of information about consumers, markets, and the effectiveness of marketing decisions. A study found that companies used marketing research for many things including, in descending order of popularity, the following:

- Measurement of market potential
- Determination of market characteristics
- Market share analysis
- Sales analysis
- Studies of business trends
- Competitive product studies
- Short-range forecasting (up to one year)
- New product acceptance and potential
- Long-range forecasting (more than one year)
- Pricing studies
- Testing of existing products
- Establishing of sales quotas and territories
- Measurement of advertising effectiveness

Most marketing research consists of making a survey of a particular sample of people by asking them to complete a QUESTION-NAIRE. This is usually done by personal interview, by mail, or by telephone.

In research, the horizon recedes as we advance, and is no nearer at 60 than it was at 20. As the power of endurance weakens with age, the urgency of the pursuit grows more intense . . . and research is always incomplete.

Mark Pattison (1813–1884)

These surveys may be individual projects (called "ad hoc research") carried out by a company's own marketing-research department or by a marketing research agency. Some surveys run by professional marketing-research firms use a regular panel of consumers or retail stores to keep a continuous eye on the movement of goods (see **A.C. NIELSEN**).

Marketing research firms like to talk of their track record; for example, when their polls say a market for a new product is favorable, they are accurate X% of the time. The most important thing about that statistic is that even the marketing research firms themselves admit that their polls are inaccurate some of the time.

Marketing research is not limited to consumer and industrial markets. Politicians and social scientists also benefit from it, although when used for such purposes it is usually called "opinion polling" or "social research."

Marketing research has become a recognized profession in recent years; the Market Research Society (MRS) has some 5,000 members worldwide. It publishes a monthly newsletter and the more learned *Journal of the Market Research Society.*

Market research is like driving along looking in the rear-view mirror. You are studying what has gone.

Anita Roddick, founder of The Body Shop

MARKET SEGMENTATION

It is generally more satisfactory to market products to a group of consumers who have similar characteristics, wants, and needs than to the general undifferentiated public. The match between what the consumer wants and what the manufacturer offers is then likely to be closer. Groups of consumers with quite detailed characteristics in common are called market segments, and the process of identifying them is called market segmentation.

Markets may be segmented in many different ways, depending on the insight or perceptiveness of the marketer. Consumer market segments are commonly based on the following kinds of characteristics:

- Demographic: housing targeted at the over-60s; Porsche cars for men with very high incomes.

- Geographic: country, state, region. A company may choose to sell its products in selected areas, or it may sell different products in different areas. Nestlé markets Nescafé in both the United States and the United Kingdom. Its decaffeinated freeze-dried Taster's Choice brand is not distributed in the United Kingdom, although the company does market a (different) decaffeinated coffee there.

- Psychographic: social class, LIFESTYLE, personality. Manufacturers of clothes, furniture, food products, cosmetics, soft drinks, and cars give great attention to market segments based on these variables.

- Use: occasion, user status, user rate. There is a summer barbecue market, as well as a charter flight market, a health food market, and so on. There are potential user, first-time user, and regular user markets, and there are markets segmented into light, medium, and heavy users.

Industrial markets are frequently segmented by type of organization (such as manufacturing, governmental, agricultural) or by type of goods required (such as raw materials, installations, services).

A market segment must meet certain standards if it is to be the focus of a marketing effort:

- Its size and purchasing power must be substantial enough to promise a profitable return.
- It must be accessible.
- It must have future as well as present viability.
- It must respond differently to marketing efforts.

Market share

A measure of a company's marketing success: its sales expressed as a percentage of total sales in a given market. It is looked on as a key indicator of competitive strength vis-à-vis rival companies' market shares.

One of the major differences between Japanese companies and companies in Europe and the United States is the degree of emphasis they place on market share. For Japanese companies, market share is at least as significant as profit; for Western companies, it is not.

Defining the boundaries of a MARKET (in order to calculate market share) can be difficult. Is the market share for a firm's instant coffee to be calculated with respect to the sales of all instant coffee, or of all coffee, or of all hot drinks (including tea)? The significance of a company's market share depends critically on what market is being shared.

The meek shall inherit the earth, but they'll never increase market share.

William McGowan, ex-chairman of MCI

Mark-up pricing

A pricing technique widely used by retailers, whereby a product's selling price is set by adding a certain percentage to its cost price (that is, marking it up).

Mass communication

An old-fashioned term for the use of the mass media (nationwide newspapers, radio, and television) for communicating with an audience.

> It's just called The Bible now. We dropped the word Holy to give it more mass-market appeal.
>
> Spokesperson, Hodder & Stoughton, publishers

Mass market

The opposite of a segmented market (see MARKET SEGMENTATION): the market in its entirety. Fewer and fewer products are expected to appeal to a mass market, so fewer and fewer products need MASS COMMUNICATION.

McCann Erickson

An international ADVERTISING AGENCY owned by the INTERPUBLIC group.

Media

The vehicles that carry ADVERTISING (among other things): television, radio, newspapers, magazines, billboards, and posters. The mass media are those vehicles that reach a national audience.

Freedom of the press is freedom to print such of the proprietor's prejudices as the advertisers don't object to.

Hannen Swaffer

MEDIA ANALYSIS

The study of the effectiveness of various media in reaching an audience. Finding answers to questions such as the following:

- How many people who buy a magazine look at the back cover, the inside front cover, the center-spread, and so on?
- How many people driving past a BILLBOARD at 60 mph can read print six feet high?
- How many people stay awake long enough to see the credits for the late-night movie?

MEDIA BROKER

An agency that buys media space (TV time, magazine pages, and so on) "in bulk" from a television station or a publisher. The broker then sells the space to a number of clients in smaller bits. This practice grew first in countries like France that are dominated by a small number of powerful media groups, but it has spread widely as a way of exploiting economies of scale. Some of the biggest media brokers are owned by advertising agencies, eager to redress what they see as an imbalance of power between their clients and the media barons.

MEDIA BUYING

The purchase of time or space in MEDIA for the showing of advertisements. This task is usually delegated to a specialist media buyer inside each ADVERTISING AGENCY. However, more and more specialist companies are setting up as media buyers. Their services are then used by agencies that do not have their own media departments.

In recent years a number of advertising agencies have pooled their media-buying departments in order to buy space (or time) in even bigger bulk from newspapers and radio or television stations. Through the even bigger discounts that this gives them, they reap further economies of scale.

One danger in all this is that individual agencies will reveal more than they wish to other agencies about the media-buying strategies of their clients.

MEDIA PLAN

The decisions made by advertisers about which media to use for an ADVERTISING CAMPAIGN. This is a question of making the most effective use of each medium within the limits of the media budget.

Media planners must know how best to reach their TARGET AUDIENCE: which magazines or newspapers such an audience reads, which television programs they watch, and so on. They must then work out the percentage of the TARGET MARKET that they hope will see the campaign; the number of times during the campaign they want each of those people to see it; and the cost of reaching them (see CPM).

MERCHANDISING

Merchandising involves the whole range of activities — displays, special promotions, shelf arrangements — that can be used to increase the sales of goods through retail outlets.

ME-TOO

A PRODUCT modeled consciously on a successful competitor: the type of product that appears on a MARKET with no differentiating features from existing products. Me-too products can be seen as an indication of the successful marketing of the products that are being copied. Such products usually have a short life and are quickly forgotten. Sometimes they are produced by well-known companies.

MIDDLEMAN

Any member of a DISTRIBUTION CHANNEL; someone who operates between the manufacturer and the consumer.

MILKING

A marketing strategy that aims to make as much profit from a PRODUCT in as short a time as possible, with no regard to its long-term future. Milking is often an appropriate strategy for marketing products associated with a FAD — toys, dolls, and various accessories, for example.

3M — the Minnesota Mining and Manufacturing Company — is a misnomer. In the twentieth century 3M has done little mining, and the firm is more famous for its Scotch tape than for anything in Minnesota.

MISSIONARY SELLING

A technique used by a company to support its wholesalers' or distributors' sales forces. A publisher's representative (the missionary salesperson) might visit teachers, for example, to dispense information about the company's new books that relate to specific fields of study. The teachers in turn recommend the books to their students, who then buy them from nearby bookstores that have purchased stock from the distributors' sales representative.

From noodles to atomic power.

Mitsubishi slogan

MOTHER-IN-LAW RESEARCH

The sort of **MARKETING RESEARCH** that involves asking questions casually of a few friends, colleagues, and family, including your mother-in-law. Useful when wishing to confirm preconceived attitudes.

MOTIVATIONAL RESEARCH

A form of **MARKETING RESEARCH** pioneered by Ernest Dichter. Using techniques like word association, sentence completion, and ink-blot interpretation, he tried to discover consumers' underlying attitudes toward products.

Motivational research into air travel led advertisers to emphasize its time-saving aspects rather than its safety, since an appeal to safety merely aroused people's irrational fear of flying.

Research into consumer attitudes to prunes revealed that their shrunken, wrinkled appearance reminded people of old age. The marketing solution to this problem for prune producers was to launch a new product: bottled prune juice.

MULTIBRAND STRATEGY

The practice of carrying many brands within one **PRODUCT LINE;** a strategy developed and practiced by Procter & Gamble, for example, with its 24 different brands of detergents. Multibrand strategy has several objectives:

- It is a means of obtaining greater shelf space than one's competitors in retail outlets.
- It is a way of dealing with "brand switchers," customers who like to try a different brand from time to time.

- It is a way of dealing with would-be competitors, leaving them no gaps in the MARKET.

- It is a way of segmenting the market, providing brands that may develop their own loyal followers.

- It can serve to create a degree of competition among company brand managers, and keep them on their toes.

NATIONAL LAUNCH

The method of introducing a new product into a **MARKET** by making it available throughout the entire market at one time rather than by distributing it gradually, area by area. (See also **LAUNCH**)

NETWORK MARKETING

A new method of selling that essentially takes the well-known Tupperware party formula to the streets. Network marketing is particularly appropriate for selling such items as costume jewelry. One practitioner described network marketing as having three essential elements: The **SALESPERSON** (1) wears the **PRODUCT**; (2) carries the catalogue constantly; (3) talks about the business everywhere and all the time. This practitioner claims to have sold jewelry this way even at a supermarket checkout and in a doctor's waiting room.

The key to the network marketing concept is to find other people to sell the product — with a commission granted on the new person's sales. This has led to the criticism that network marketing focuses more on finding salespeople than on actually selling the merchandise.

NEW PRODUCT DEVELOPMENT

The range of activities involved in conceiving, developing, and launching a new **PRODUCT** into a **MARKET**. Because most firms introduce new products frequently and continually in order to retain competitive advantage, new product development is a critically important process. Failure rates are high. Only about half the new products placed on the market become commercially viable.

There are seven steps in new product development:

1. New product strategy   2. Idea generation

3. Screening   6. Testing
4. Business analysis   7. Commercialization
5. Development

Nestlé's trademark of birds in a nest was designed by founder Henri Nestlé, a research chemist who started the Swiss food company in 1866. (In Swiss-German Nestlé means "little nest.")

NICHE MARKETING

See CONCENTRATED SEGMENTATION

A. C. NIELSEN

A company founded in 1939 and now the most famous marketing research firm in the world. Its services include the Nielsen Index, a measure of shopping patterns established by a continuous monitoring of sales from retail food outlets, drug stores, liquor stores, and cash-and-carry wholesalers. Nielsen is also well known for its measurement of television audiences.

NONPROFIT MARKETING

The application of marketing to the nonprofit sector. Strictly speaking, entities such as symphony orchestras, national art galleries, universities, and the armed forces are not in the business of seeking profits. But they have a relationship with the public, and to nourish that relationship they need to use marketing techniques. Museums run little shops; the armed forces advertise for recruits.

The name Nylon was created by its inventor, DuPont, and has no significance whatsoever.

Odd-even Pricing

A pricing convention used in retailing whereby a product's price is not rounded up, but is left as a figure ending in a five or a nine (both "odd" numbers). Thus $24.95 is used in preference to $25.

This odd convention persists even though it has never been proved that consumers actually believe odd-priced goods are better values than even-priced goods.

Off-card Rate

The selling of advertising space in a newspaper, or of time on a television channel, at a price below that quoted on the medium's RATE CARD.

Off-the-rack Research

MARKETING RESEARCH that used data previously collected by someone other than the researcher. Four main types of off-the-rack material are used:

- Published sources
- Data regularly collected and sold by marketing research companies (see SYNDICATED RESEARCH)
- Data on specialist subjects regularly collected and sold by marketing research companies (see SPECIALIST RESEARCH)
- Data commissioned from syndicated surveys (see OMNIBUS RESEARCH)

Ogilvy & Mather

An ADVERTISING AGENCY nurtured into prominence largely by David Ogilvy, a legend of the advertising industry famous for his pithy comments. The agency is now part of the WPP group.

OMNIBUS RESEARCH

The results of surveys that are based on questionnaires sent out regularly to a panel of respondents by marketing researchers. Space on the QUESTIONNAIRE is sold and made available to firms that have specific marketing-research needs.

It is called "omnibus" research because it carries a number of different passengers.

OMNICOM

A publicly owned U.S. advertising agency group that is structured on much the same lines as INTERPUBLIC. Omnicom owns two worldwide advertising agencies, BBDO and DDB NEEDHAM.

ONE-STOP SHOPPING

A strategy commonly found among financial services firms and consultants in the 1980s, based on a belief that customers liked to buy services as they buy groceries: all in one place. So groups like SAATCHI & SAATCHI ballooned, believing that clients who bought ADVERTISING might also buy, say, MARKETING RESEARCH and a human resource consultant while they were on the premises. For the most part it did not work like that. Customers remained faithful to specialist providers of services and many one-stop shops have been disbanded.

OPEN-ENDED QUESTION

A question that requires more than a response to structured categories such as "yes," "no," or "don't know." For example:

- What features do you look for when purchasing a new car?
- What factors do you think are important in preparing meals for your family?

Particularly important for certain sorts of MARKETING RESEARCH.

OPINION LEADER

A person who influences the purchasing behavior of others, often by word of mouth or example. Opinion leaders are not necessarily the first to adopt a new product or idea (see **INNOVATOR**), but their acceptance of it is vitally important to its ultimate success.

If these people can be reached by selected media advertising, then the multiplier effect widens public acceptance of the **PRODUCT** far beyond the media's immediate audience.

OPINION POLL

Consumer research concerned specifically with politics. Opinion polls are now an integral part of political campaigns in most parts of the world. Most polls are commissioned by members of the **MEDIA** for consumption by the public, but political parties and candidates also commission opinion polls to help them with their campaign strategies.

Some marketing research agencies have become famous for their opinion polling; examples include Gallup, Harris, MORI, and Elmo Roper. They use various techniques, from telephone calls to face-to-face interviews, with population samples that rarely exceed a couple of thousand. Their capacity to be accurate is undoubted; their ability to predict electoral outcomes is unpredictable.

I could prove God, statistically.

George Gallup

OPTIMISTIC STRIVER

A type of consumer unique to southern Europe: Greece, Italy, Portugal, and Spain (see **LIFESTYLE**).

ORANGE GOODS

A category of consumer goods — items of clothing, for example — that consumers change at a moderate rate either because of wear-and-tear or because of changing fashion. To be contrasted with FAST-MOVING CONSUMER GOODS, which are characterized by a much quicker turnover.

ORGANIZATIONAL BUYING

The way in which organizations, as opposed to individuals, identify, evaluate, and choose the products they buy.

A car manufacturer, for example, buys hundreds of components from accessory suppliers. The company's negotiations with such suppliers may start at the early stages of the research and development of a new model and continue on until that model is replaced.

OVERKILL

A heavy marketing effort that produces diminishing returns because it engenders a hostile rather than a favorable reaction among consumers.

OWN LABEL

See DEALER BRAND

PACKAGED GOODS

Consumer goods that are packaged by their manufacturer and not sold loose. Such goods include most food, cosmetics, and cleaning products. Despite the hygienic advantages of packaged goods, many consumers still seek out unpackaged alternatives of such goods as fruit and vegetables, for example. More and more producers of packaged goods are taking environmental concerns into account when designing PACKAGING.

PACKAGING

Today packaging has become an integral part of many products. Originally the packaging may have been designed to protect the PRODUCT, but now it carries out a range of additional functions.

- Convenient dispensing of contents (liquid soaps, glue, toothpaste, and so forth)
- Conveying important information about the contents (sometimes required by law)
- Promoting and advertising the product itself.

Through DESIGN and labeling, a package can become as important as what it contains. People may still like to buy boiled candy in brown paper bags, but they want their designer chocolates in something a bit more glamorous.

PAIRED COMPARISONS

A technique used in MARKETING RESEARCH. It asks consumers to rank their preferences among different products. They are presented with a pair of products or brands and asked to choose the one they prefer. Soft drink research might use the following pairs.

Coca-Cola — Pepsi-Cola	Pepsi-Cola — 7 Up
Coca-Cola — 7 Up	Pepsi-Cola — Dr Pepper
Coca-Cola — Dr Pepper	Pepsi-Cola — Fresca
Dr Pepper — Fresca	7 Up — Dr Pepper
7 Up — Fresca	Coca-Cola — Fresca

The results will show the number of times each brand was preferred in comparison with another. Fresca, for example, might be preferred in every pairing and receive a rating of four, Pepsi might be preferred three times, and so on. The final figures reveal an order of brand preference.

Panel

A sample of consumers who record their purchases over time for the purposes of MARKETING RESEARCH (see DIARY PANEL). Audits attempt to measure consumer patterns from the viewpoint of the seller; panels attempt to measure consumer patterns from the viewpoint of the buyer. The picture is rarely the same.

Pareto principle

Sometimes referred to as the 80/20 rule, it is more an observation of a common occurrence: that 80% of one thing comes from 20% of another. For example, many companies seem to derive 80% of their profits from 20% of their PRODUCT LINE; many sell 80% of their output through 20% of their distribution outlets.

The principle was first enunciated by a nineteenth-century Italian economist by the name of Pareto. But he first applied it to the wealth of nations: 80% of the wealth belonged to 20% of the population, regardless of the absolute wealth of the nation. From that he concluded that the only way to spread wealth was to redistribute it; creating more of it would simply retain the same 80/20 ownership ratio.

> *20% of any group of salesmen will always produce 90% of the sales.*
>
> Robert Townsend's version of the Pareto principle, quoted in
> *Up the Organization*

PATCHWORK PRODUCT

A **PRODUCT** that has so many problems that no sooner is one solved than another appears.

> *Sales resistance is the triumph of mind over patter.*
>
> Anon

PATENT

A type of protection for intellectual property, registered patents protect inventions from being copied. Large pharmaceutical firms and consumer electronics manufacturers, which are heavily dependent on R&D, own literally thousands of patents registered with relevant authorities around the world.

PAYMENT SYSTEM

An increasingly important part of the selling process is the provision of convenient payment terms and conditions. For the sale of **FAST-MOVING CONSUMER GOODS**, electronic payment systems have helped speed up progress through the supermarket checkout, and laser technology has permitted the speedy production of detailed invoices.

For consumer durables that are purchased only occasionally, the availability of customer credit is much more important. For regular but infrequent purchases (such as magazine subscriptions) techniques like the negative option (which continues the subscription into the next period unless the customer says "no") ease the purchasing process.

PENETRATION

The percentage of a TARGET MARKET that has bought a particular product at least once.

PENETRATION STRATEGY

The use of low prices and heavy advertising to increase MARKET SHARE. Such a strategy is appropriate when a company has a PRODUCT in a MARKET supplied with products that are relatively similar to one another.

For such a strategy to be attempted, the market will have to be large enough for the company to be able to sustain relatively low profit margins. Penetration strategy has the added advantage of deterring potential new entrants, who may view the market as having limited possibilities for profit.

PERCEPTION

The process by which an individual receives, selects, and interprets information. Marketers and advertising specialists are particularly interested in the phenomenon of perception; they want to find the signals that will produce in the consumer a favorable view or perception of their product (its IMAGE).

When the signals are right, ADVERTISING can be very powerful; people's perceptions of products owe much more to skillful advertising than they do to any intrinsic or exclusive qualities that the products may possess.

PERCEPTUAL MAPPING

A technique borrowed from psychology that helps marketers understand the structure of a MARKET. Consumers develop an

IMAGE of a PRODUCT based on its particular features, on its benefits (real or imagined), or on its price. These perceptions can be identified (see QUALITATIVE RESEARCH), and products can be plotted on a graph or map. The closer two brands are on the map, the closer they are competitively.

If research has also identified the characteristics of an "ideal" product, then the closer a brand is to that point, the more likely it is to be preferred over others. Gaps on the map may represent potential market opportunities.

PERSONAL SELLING

Direct face-to-face communication between a buyer and a seller. Personal selling is as old as marketing itself (see DIRECT MARKETING). In marketing INDUSTRIAL GOODS it is generally more important than ADVERTISING because here the SALESPERSON must meet the particular (and perhaps unique) requirements of each customer.

PILOT

A trial undertaken on a modest scale in order to test the feasibility of something much bigger. Thus a pilot plant is a small production operation set up to test new processes before a complete factory is commissioned. Similarly, a pilot questionnaire is used in tests before being honed for a full marketing-research survey.

PIMS

See PROFIT IMPACT OF MARKET STRATEGY

POINT OF SALE

The place where the whole marketing effort — the sale — culminates. The term usually refers to a retail store, but with the advent of self-service and the technological revolution, it may now mean a checkout counter or a through-the-wall bank teller machine. It can also be inside the customer's own home. So-called home shopping allows customers to make purchases in their pajamas via an interface with their television screens.

He who has a thing to sell
And goes and whispers in a well
Is not so apt to get the dollars
As he who climbs a tree and hollers.

Anon

PORTFOLIO ANALYSIS

A concept borrowed from the investment community and now used by marketers to evaluate a company's products in order to decide how best to allocate company resources among them. There are several different methods of product portfolio analysis in current use, including the following.

- The Boston Consulting Group's Growth/Share Matrix
- The GENERAL ELECTRIC BUSINESS SCREEN
- Shell's Directional Policy Matrix

All involve an analysis of the profitability, prospects, and investment requirements of the company's products.

A company's ideal PRODUCT MIX consists of a balance between products that are very profitable and those that are expected to become very profitable. The cash coming in from the former is available for investment in support of the latter.

Like the planning process, portfolio analysis can be applied at many different levels of a business. In a large multiproduct company it is applied at top-management level to the company's STRATEGIC BUSINESS UNITS (separate divisions, each of which handles one of the company's product lines). Then, within each SBU, managers can apply portfolio analysis further to analyze the specific products under their responsibility.

POSITIONING

The attempt by marketers to give a PRODUCT a certain identity or IMAGE so that it will be perceived to have distinctive features or benefits relative to competing products.

Suppose a shopper goes to a SUPERMARKET set on buying a dishwashing detergent that is kind to the hands. Chances are that his or her choice will be Ivory Liquid, a product that is firmly positioned, vis-à-vis the shopper, in the "gentle to hands" position.

If the shopper had wanted a simple, functional detergent at a cheap price, then he or she probably would have chosen the supermarket's own BRAND. Dealer brands hold the "reliable and cheaper" position in the market.

But suppose there is another brand of dishwashing detergent on the shelf: Wash-Up. Its label says it is kind to hands, and it is competitive in price. But it does not sell because the brand name does not mean these things to the consumer.

If the marketers of Wash-Up do not want to see their product fail, they must "position" it. They have two choices.

1. Because they know Wash-Up is chemically gentle to hands, they can try to implant the name Wash-Up in the minds of consumers as being such, in direct competition with Ivory.

   The chances of success with this strategy are slim. Once a consumer has associated one brand name with a position, the bonding tends to last, to the effective exclusion of all others. With massive effort Pepsi has managed to take a share of the cola market from Coca-Cola, but it has not ousted Coke as the name that means cola.

   Similarly, Avis challenged Hertz in the rental car market by declaring: "We're number two. We try harder." Avis did well, but Hertz remained the market leader.

2. Alternatively, Wash-Up's marketers are more likely to be successful if they can find a position in the MARKET unlike that of any other brand. They might discover, for example,

that changing lifestyles had created an unfilled "masculine" position for the man about the house who also cleans the pots. Their marketing efforts would then be directed at creating a dishwashing detergent for men.

In markets where almost every conceivable position seems to have been taken, this strategy would not be easy. In the shampoo market, for example, there are shampoos for dry hair, greasy hair, frequently washed hair, fair hair, dark hair, gray hair, baby hair, and so on.

Poster

An advertising medium that forms a striking part of the landscape of most modern cities, although it accounts for less than 10% of all advertising expenditure.

Smaller posters are usually printed on paper and pasted onto visible parts of buildings. Larger posters — called BILLBOARDS — are stuck on freestanding sites (called supersites) created especially for the purpose, usually by the side of major highways.

In some cases posters have developed into an art form. One poster advertising the Sony Walkman was so popular that (much to Sony's fury) it was simply removed from most public sites as a collector's item. In large cities it is common to see the entire side of a multistory apartment block covered with a single advertisement that attracts attention by its scale, if nothing else. Other posters are sculpted in three dimensions, often incorporating simulations of the advertised product to attract attention and generate interest.

PR

See PUBLIC RELATIONS

Premium offer

A form of sales promotion that offers a customer the opportunity to obtain one product either free or at an attractive price by purchasing another. The premium device is particularly popular with cosmetics manufacturers; purchasers of a new after-shave lotion, for example, often walk away from the store with a piece of luggage or a towel that dwarfs their purchase.

Pre-testing

A marketing research technique used to predict the effectiveness of an advertisement before it is (expensively) released. An **ADVERTISING AGENCY** will define the objectives of a piece of media advertising and then test it, using group discussion, to determine the extent to which the objectives will be realized.

Print advertising is sometimes tested by split runs, in which different advertisements are alternated and readers' responses to each are measured and compared.

The Schwerin test is a recognized method for testing television and radio commercials. Before being exposed to the commercial, respondents are asked to choose a **BRAND**. After seeing the advertisement, they are asked to choose again; any change in their selection is considered a measure of the effectiveness of the commercial.

Price discrimination

When intermediaries or industrial buyers purchase products of similar quality and in similar quantity, they expect to buy them on the same terms. If the seller favors one or more of its customers, and the difference in price cannot be justified in cost terms, then under the law an offense has been committed.

Price sensitive

The effect that an increase (or decrease) in price has on the sales of a **PRODUCT** or service. A product is said to be highly price sensitive if a small change in price results in a large change in sales. In general, low-price commodity-type goods are very price sensitive; high-price luxury goods are not.

Price war

The situation in which firms try to gain MARKET SHARE by cutting their prices below the prices of their competitors. If the competitors follow suit, this can lead to a vicious spiral in which many firms lose money; some may even go bankrupt. To avoid this, some manufacturers fix (for their own internal purposes) a rock-bottom price that they vow never to go below, even in the most bitter price war.

U.S. airlines and U.K. package-tour operators are notorious for engaging in price wars. Not entirely coincidentally, both industries have also seen more than their share of bankruptcies.

Pricing

The crucial art of deciding what price to charge for a PRODUCT or service. Set it too high and nobody will buy; set it too low and it will not be profitable. (See also MILKING)

There are as many methods to determine prices as there are ways to skin a cat. Perhaps the most common is to add the fixed cost per unit to the variable cost per unit and then add on a percentage for the profit. But this involves guesswork, as the fixed cost per unit cannot be known until the manufacturer knows how many units will be sold, and that cannot be known until the price has been fixed.

If the MARKET allows, a simpler way to determine price is to follow the price leader: the market participant who "leads" prices up and down. The newcomer needs to follow a discrete distance behind the market leader with a price that is competitively less.

In certain industries manufacturers are given "pricing points" that they have to stay below if they are to get the business at all. For example, a fashion retailer will decide that a certain type and style of blouse will sell at no more than $29.95 and so will work backward from that amount, subtracting the profit and value-added to each stage in the manufacturing and distribution process in order to arrive at a pricing point to give to the manufacturer.

PRIME TIME

That time of day (or night) when there are most viewers watching television or listening to the radio. The MEDIA charge extra for advertisements shown in prime time.

On network television, prime time refers to the period in the evening between 8:00 and 11:00. On commercial radio, though, prime time is often in the morning, during what is called "drive time."

PRIVATE LABEL

See DEALER BRAND

PRODUCT

Anything that can be offered to a MARKET that might satisfy a need or a want. It may be an object, a service, a place, an organization, or an idea.

Products can be thought about on three levels.

- Every product has a core benefit (for example, soaps and detergents make things clean). This is known as the "core product."
- Products also have BRAND, PACKAGING, QUALITY, and style.
- Beyond these direct attributes there is the "augmented product," which includes the GUARANTEE, AFTER-SALES SERVICE, installation, delivery, credit terms, and so on.

PRODUCT CLASS

A term applied to the largest grouping of products that have similar functions. Cigarettes, automobiles, and microcomputers each are a product class.

PRODUCT DIFFERENTIATION

The practice of making one product distinguishable from others. Products may be differentiated by QUALITY, price, styling, and service.

Because multiple products perform similar functions in virtually every product class, some differentiation is necessary. Many a company must distinguish its brands not only from the brands of competing firms, but also from one another.

PRODUCT ELIMINATION

The orderly process of withdrawing a PRODUCT from the market (also called product deletion). Products do not live forever. For most of them profitable life is short; even the most long-lived products can eventually go into decline.

Many companies do not like to face this fact. Through poor management or nostalgia they often continue to offer products even when the products are consistently losing money. An unprofitable product is not necessarily an overall liability, however. In some cases it may contribute to the ease of selling other products. Car dealers, for example, may consider that their reputations for excellent service are enhanced by stocking accessories for old models, products that in themselves are unprofitable to the manufacturer.

If they have been familiar brands, products marked for deletion may be "harvested" — that is, made to produce a short-term profit — before they are withdrawn.

PRODUCTIVITY

The relationship between sales and expenditure, a too-often ignored subject in MARKETING. Marketers have traditionally used resources without looking very closely at the relationship between that use and resulting sales. Is the cost of increasing the amount of ADVERTISING going to be less than the extra revenue from the resultant increase in sales? If not, then what is the point of it? There may be a point, but the question has to be asked.

PRODUCT LIFE CYCLE

A concept that has attracted marketers for many years. Using a biological analogy for products: they are born, introduced to the MARKET (in a sort of product bar mitzvah), grow in sales, mature (sales growth stops), and then decline (sales fall off).

The analogy is sometimes extended also to markets; they too are born, grow, and die, in what is referred to as a "demand life cycle."

It is tempting to deduce from this that it is possible to predict movements in sales according to the "time of life" of a particular product. Different marketing strategies can thus be developed for different stages in a product's life cycle.

Critics of the life-cycle approach argue that the shape of the sales curve, far from being preordained, is a function of the marketing effort that is put into the product: hence the life cycle has no value as a forecasting tool.

Furthermore, critics point to brands that appear to demonstrate no life cycle. Look at the following table of brand names that were number one in their respective product classes in 1933 and were still number one 60 years later.

Brand Names	Product
Campbell's	Soup
Coca-Cola	Soft drinks
Del Monte	Canned fruit
Eastman Kodak	Cameras, film
Gillette	Razors
Ivory	Soap
Wrigley	Chewing gum

Source: Interbrand.

PRODUCT LINE

A group of closely related products marketed by the same company. Companies can support one or many product lines, and product lines can contain few or many products. Heinz has a product line with more than 57 varieties, while Procter & Gamble has something like 57 product lines, including beauty care products, chemicals, detergents, disposable diapers, and so on.

The number of products within a product line is related to the number of different consumer segments that a company has been able to identify and supply.

PRODUCT MANAGEMENT

See BRAND MANAGEMENT

PRODUCT MARKET

A company's PRODUCT LINE is frequently sold to several different classes of customer. Each of these classes is considered a product market and has distinct requirements. A line of food products, for example, may be sold to the retail market (grocery outlets), to the catering market (restaurants and hotels), and to the institutional market (schools, hospitals, military installations, prisons). Each product market requires a different marketing approach.

PRODUCT MIX

This is the whole range of products offered to consumers by a single company. Product mix is described in the following terms:

- Width. The number of product lines a company offers.
- Length. The number of brands of each PRODUCT; Procter & Gamble, for example, has several brands of soap.
- Depth. The number of variants that each brand has; soap may come in hand size, bath size, guest size, family size, and so on.

- Consistency. The extent to which the product lines are related.

PROFIT CENTER

An organizational unit or function within a company that is charged with producing a profit.

PROFIT IMPACT OF MARKET STRATEGY

An extensive database that throws some light on the factors that bring about different rates of return on investment (ROI) in different industries. Commonly known by its acronym, PIMS.

PROMOTION

In MARKETING, a special effort to increase the sales of a PRODUCT. This may be through a one-off advertising campaign, through special displays at trade shows and retail outlets, or through competitions broadcast in the MEDIA.

PROMOTIONAL BUDGET

An estimate of the likely cost of a PROMOTION.

PROSPECT

Any individual to whom a marketer aims to sell a PRODUCT. Marketers do not set out to prospect for a mine; they set out to mine for a prospect.

PSYCHOGRAPHICS

A system for segmenting consumer markets that is based on social class (see A/B/C1), LIFESTYLE, and personality.

PUBLICIS-FCB

A close association between two advertising agencies: Publicis, founded in 1926 by the acknowledged father of French advertising, Marcel Bleustein-Blanchet, and FCB, founded by the father of modern U.S. advertising, Albert Lasker. Until 1943, FCB was known as Lord & Thomas, then one of the most famous names in advertising. The name was changed when Lasker retired.

The U.S. and French agencies formed an affiliation in 1988. Publicis was the biggest agency in France; FCB added clout in the United States, the most important advertising market in the world.

PUBLIC RELATIONS

"The means by which an organization tries to develop a mutual understanding between itself and its public," according to the Institute of Public Relations. Contrary to popular belief, public relations (PR) is a two-way means of communication, as much about listening as about telling.

While much PR work is concerned with handling press conferences and press releases, PR covers a wide range of activities, from preparing in-house newsletters to negotiating sponsorship deals. A company's relations with governments, with consumer groups, trade unions, and investors may all appropriately involve PR.

Public relations can be carried out by in-house public relations officers (PROs), company employees specifically charged with the task, or it can be subcontracted to a firm of PR specialists. (Many big companies do both.)

PUBLICITY

The attention of the public. "The only truly bad publicity is no publicity" goes the old saying, although it is not certain that the U.K. royal family (for one example) would entirely agree with that.

Companies spend a lot of time and money seeking publicity for their products. They woo journalists and editors and take them on foreign trips. And they sponsor sports and arts events that are themselves sure to attract a lot of publicity.

PUSH AND PULL STRATEGIES

Two different ways to move consumer goods through a DISTRIBUTION CHANNEL. Most companies have to use a push strategy to move products, persuading each member in the distribution channel to stock them.

A large, rich company, however, may be able to choose a pull strategy. By investing large sums of money in ADVERTISING and sales promotion, such a company can create consumer demand for its PRODUCT. That demand then acts as a pull to draw the product through the distribution system.

PYRAMID SELLING

A system of selling goods (often household goods such as cleaning products or cosmetics) by setting up a pyramid consisting of layers and layers of agents. The first agent sells a stock of the products to a number of other agents (for a commission), and each of them sells to a number of others (again for a commission), and so, in theory, ad infinitum.

By the time the pyramid has built up into a reasonable size there are hundreds of agents all over the place, and there is no way they can sell all the products they hold at a price that will leave them with a profit. In some countries pyramid selling has been made illegal.

QUALITATIVE RESEARCH

MARKETING RESEARCH that is designed to gain insights into a consumer's attitude, perception, and motivation. Such research makes no attempt to come up with statistically measured results.

Its methods are chiefly group discussion and **DEPTH INTERVIEW**, and the number of respondents involved in a research session is small, perhaps fewer than 50.

Qualitative research is widely used in **NEW PRODUCT DEVELOPMENT** to elicit consumers' views of what are desirable and undesirable features of the **PRODUCT**. It is also frequently used in the early stages of the development of a major research project in order to give the researchers a general feel for the situation.

Quality is free.

Phil Crosby

QUALITY

The most-discussed subject in management in the 1980s, with almost as many interpretations as discussion participants. Quality was something that Japanese products and industrial processes had but that Western ones by and large did not. The quality approach to business and industry starts with the point of view of the customer. From there it aims to provide products and services that exceed customers' expectations. Quality is a measure of the extent to which this effort succeeds.

It pays to give most products an image of quality; a first-class ticket.

David Ogilvy

QUANTITATIVE RESEARCH

MARKETING RESEARCH that uses sampling techniques in order to arrive at quantitative results. This research reveals what proportion of the population owns video recorders, for example, or watches "L.A. Law."

AGB, a research firm, suggests that there are only a few basic questions underlying all quantitative marketing research:

- Who are you?
- What do you buy?
- Where do you buy?
- How much?
- At what price?
- When?
- What else could you have bought?
- Where else could you have bought it?

QUANTITY DISCOUNT

A price reduction given to a customer who buys in large quantities; the larger the quantity purchased, the larger the discounts.

Quantity discounts are usually offered by manufacturers to wholesalers, but they are also offered by wholesalers to retailers. Retail grocery chains negotiate quantity discounts directly with manufacturers because they buy in such large quantities.

QUESTIONNAIRE

The primary tool of MARKETING RESEARCH, a device for delivering questions to respondents and recording their answers. It has four main purposes:

1. To collect relevant data
2. To make data comparable
3. To minimize bias in the asking of questions and the recording of answers

4. To frame questions in a varied and interesting way so that respondents will answer without resentment

The design of the questionnaire is of great importance to the success of research. It must cover the ground without being too long, and the questions must be easy to understand and not ambiguous. To get the questionnaire right, therefore, it is usual to try out a **PILOT** before the final questionnaire is released for field work.

With a pilot, interviewers conduct the interview in the normal way and note any difficulties that arise. The feedback from the trial is then used to redesign those parts of the questionnaire that cause problems.

I keep six honest serving men
(They taught me all I know)
Their names are What and Why and When
And How and Where and Who.

Rudyard Kipling

Quota sample

A selection of respondents for a piece of **MARKETING RESEARCH** such that age, sex, class, and so on are represented in the same proportion as in the population as a whole.

RANDOM SAMPLE

A population sample selected in such a way that each member of the population has an equal chance of being chosen. It is not easy to select such a sample because in all populations some members are less accessible than others; they may effectively make themselves unselectable by being abroad, sick, or just unwilling to participate. Hence, although marketing researchers would like to use random samples most of the time, in practice they have to rely on some self-selection in their samples.

RATE CARD

A list of advertising prices charged by a television channel, a radio station, a newspaper, or a magazine. A television rate card typically includes the cost of a 30-second spot at different times of the day. A newspaper or magazine rate card includes the cost of a full-page or half-page advertisement plus special rates for the back page or for inside the front cover.

Rate cards are used by advertising agencies in planning their use of the MEDIA. They are also of considerable interest to marketing managers who have advertising budgets to prepare.

REACH

The proportion of a total market that an advertiser wants to reach at least once in an ADVERTISING CAMPAIGN. If the TARGET MARKET is made up of about one million people and the reach is 80%, then 800,000 people will have to see the ADVERTISING over the given period.

RECALL TEST

A test used by marketing researchers to find out how much consumers remember about particular advertisements.

Unaided recall tests reveal which advertisements respondents can spontaneously remember. Aided recall tests show which advertisements they can remember from a series they are shown.

RECOMMENDED PRICE

Many manufacturers recommend a price that retailers should charge for their products. In part this is to help give price guidelines to retailers operating in the same market, but it is also used to determine what manufacturers charge retailers for goods — for example, 50% of the recommended retail price.

Fearful that retail price-cutting might create an unstable market, manufacturers in the past would refuse to supply retailers who charged less than their recommended price. But this practice has now been outlawed in most free-market economies.

RED GOODS

FAST-MOVING CONSUMER GOODS (such as food) that are consumed and replaced at a rapid rate. Compare with ORANGE GOODS and YELLOW GOODS.

REFERENCE GROUP

A social group on which consumers model their behavior. A reference group may be a bunch of friends, neighbors, or colleagues, or it may be a distant group that the consumer admires or aspires to belong to — film or rock stars, for example.

The influence of reference groups is strongest where highly conspicuous products such as clothes, cars, drinks, or high-tech equipment are involved. Marketers attempt to associate such products with the appropriate reference groups.

REGISTERED DESIGN

In order to maintain exclusive use of distinctive corporate designs — shapes, patterns, configurations, or unusual ornamentation — companies need to register them.

RELAUNCH

The reintroduction of an existing brand on to the MARKET after changes have been made to it (see also REPOSITIONING). For example, in the 1980s Colgate relaunched its Palmolive soap as a product for the health conscious. It underwent some cosmetic changes: a new, softer shade of its original green color, a more rounded shape, and new packaging.

At the end of the 1980s Nabisco relaunched Shredded Wheat without making any changes whatsoever. It simply ran a major advertising campaign that emphasized the dietary qualities of the old product: high fiber, low fat, and no added sugar or salt.

REPERTOIRE

The group of brands within a PRODUCT CLASS that a consumer considers acceptable: those brands that he or she will purchase occasionally. Complete BRAND LOYALTY (in which a consumer never buys anything but a particular brand of a product) is very rare.

REPOSITIONING

When a company decides that one of its products is not performing as well as it might because its original (successful) POSITIONING has invited too many competitors, the company may attempt to reposition the product by changing some features such as its PACKAGING, its price, or even its DISTRIBUTION CHANNEL.

In the 1980s both Nissan and Volkswagen repositioned their cars from low-priced to mid-priced models. One of the most dramatic repositioning successes was based on a change of distributor. The Hanes Company renamed and repackaged its line of women's hosiery and introduced it as a supermarket item. As L'eggs, Hanes pantyhose was a "runaway" success.

REPRESENTATIVE SAMPLE

See QUOTA SAMPLE

RESEARCH BRIEF

A written statement defining the objectives of a piece of MARKETING RESEARCH, as agreed between the company that is commissioning the research and the agency that is going to undertake it.

RETAILER

The place where products and consumers finally get together, the last stop on the DISTRIBUTION CHANNEL. Retailers come in many different shapes and sizes, from department stores to corner stores, from hypermarkets to flea markets. There are almost two million of them in the United States.

A man without a smiling face must not open a shop.

Chinese proverb

ROLLING LAUNCH

The process of gradually introducing a new PRODUCT into the MARKET. The first stage might consist of putting the product through a market test. If it is successful, then DISTRIBUTION might be extended, perhaps to another test area. This way the whole market will gradually be covered.

ROP

See below

RUN-OF-PAPER

Advertisements that appear in newspapers or magazines in no particular order — that is, they do not have a specified position (such as "facing contents page"). Run-of-paper (ROP) advertisements are less expensive than those that are designated a particular position. But there is a risk that the ad will end up near the back of the publication, possibly facing an article that nobody wants to read.

SAATCHI & SAATCHI

In its heyday as a teenager in the mid-1980s, this advertising and marketing group was the biggest in the world. Established in London by two brothers from Iraq, the agency became a supermarket of marketing services, growing through the purchase of companies in everything from MARKETING RESEARCH to PUBLIC RELATIONS to management consultancy.

The agency fell on hard times, partly because of the recession in the industry at the beginning of the 1990s and partly because it overstretched itself; at one time it publicly contemplated buying Midland Bank, an old-established U.K. institution. The attempt failed, but it invited ridicule.

SALES FORECAST

An estimate of how much a company hopes to sell to a MARKET, calculated separately for each PRODUCT. A sales forecast forms the basis for establishing a SALES QUOTA.

Forecasting for new products is not easy; it may have to depend on extrapolating from demand for similar products or on market tests of the product.

Forecasting sales for existing products is considerably easier but still depends on analyzing the dynamics of markets that are constantly changing. Statistical tools such as TIME-SERIES ANALYSIS and multiple-regression models (which identify the factors that influence sales) can be employed. Despite these sophisticated techniques, the fingers-in-the-wind judgments of managers and salespeople are still widely used.

Marketing is just sales with a college education.

Anon

Sales incentive

A special reward offered to a SALESPERSON for exceeding a predetermined goal. The reward may be in the form of cash, but it is increasingly common for incentives to take the form of special holidays, for example, or trips to exotic places. A number of travel agents specialize in providing "incentive travel" for large companies and their employees.

Sales letter

A letter sent to potential customers to remind them of the existence of a particular product or to alert them to the LAUNCH of a new product.

Sales literature

The collection of published material produced by a manufacturer (catalogues, sales letters, advertisements, brochures, and so on) as part of the MARKETING of its products.

Sales mix

The proportion of different products sold from within a range produced by a manufacturer. Thus a garment manufacturer may have a sales mix of 3y shirts, 2y trousers, and y jackets. If the profitability of each is known, the manufacturer can make calculations about how it wants the mix to shift.

Salesperson

Someone employed to sell products or services. The terms "sales staff" or "sales representatives" are also widely used. In some industries (stockbroking, for example) salespeople must be licensed to carry out their trade.

A salesman has got to dream, boy. It comes with the territory.

Arthur Miller, *Death of a Salesman*

SALES QUOTA

The specified targets that a company expects a SALESPERSON to reach in a given period (usually every quarter). Sales quotas are based on the company's SALES FORECAST, but they may be set higher than the forecast in order to push the sales staff harder. Salespeople's earnings are often related to the extent to which they exceed or fall short of their quotas.

---

*The smoothest thing about a used car
is the salesman.*

Anon

SALES RESPONSE FUNCTION

The relationship between likely sales volume and different levels of marketing support during a specified period of time. Other things being equal, the higher the level of marketing support (particularly of ADVERTISING and sales promotion), the more of the product is likely to be sold.

Marketing managers try to calculate sales response functions (albeit imprecisely) using a mixture of judgment, statistical analysis of past sales and marketing expenditure, and occasional experiments — for example, in a smallish television region where the results of an increase in advertising expenditure can be more easily measured.

SALES TERRITORY

The basic unit of organization of a sales force. Each SALESPERSON is assigned an exclusive territory in which to sell the company's products. It is his or her responsibility to develop and cultivate contacts in that territory and to accept credit (or blame) for the sales performance there.

Salient attribute

The aspect of a PRODUCT that is most noticeable to a consumer and by which the product tends to be judged. Margarine's salient attribute could be said to be its spreadability; a blanket's is its warmth.

Sample

A PRODUCT, sometimes specially packaged, given free to consumers in an attempt to persuade them to try something new. Samples can be delivered door-to-door, attached to other products, or handed out in a retail store. They are an effective but potentially expensive way of getting a product into the hands of consumers. The high cost is not a deterrent: Procter & Gamble is believed to have given away 20 million samples during the launch of Vidal Sassoon's Wash & Go shampoo.

The practice of giving away samples has boomed in recent years. For detergents, the sample has become the cornerstone for launching a new brand. Surveys reveal that 94% of housewives believe in samples over any other method of product introduction; 79% say it is the main reason for purchasing a new product; 71% say it is the main reason for switching brands. Television advertising lags a long way behind at 40%.

Sampling

Taking a limited number of a large population so that by studying the part something may be learned about the whole. The "population" is all those people who have the characteristics in which the researcher is interested.

Sampling has lots of sound statistical theory behind it. The larger the sample, the more accurate the result — and the greater the cost of the sampling. Because most marketing-research projects do not require very high degrees of accuracy, samples are usually small. National research on consumer goods will normally not involve more than 1,500–2,000 respondents. Minimal samples would be in the region of 300–500.

Sample participants can be selected in several ways. For studies requiring the greatest statistical validity a RANDOM SAMPLE is used, and names are obtained from an unbiased source such as a telephone directory or voting lists. For most marketing-research projects, however, samples may be chosen more selectively, as in a QUOTA SAMPLE.

SBU

See STRATEGIC BUSINESS UNIT

SCIENTIFIC MARKETING

A once-fashionable term but a misnomer; not even the most devoted marketers would claim much scientific support for their discipline. Nevertheless, scientific marketing is useful shorthand for the systematic ordering of marketing techniques in order to minimize uncertainty in an uncertain marketplace.

SCRAMBLED MERCHANDISING

An expression referring to the tendency of retailers to move away from selling specialized goods and into whatever product areas are profitable. For example, drug stores sell a lot more than drugs.

SCREENING

A process of analyzing a new product's chances of success by considering the extent to which the product has (or has not) those elements that will determine its success. For instance, screening a new pizza would involve considering how acceptable factors such as the thickness of crust, the variety of topping, or the flavor of cheese were to the market at which it was to be aimed.

SECONDARY DATA

All information used by marketing researchers that has not been gathered directly by them: the opposite of primary data. It includes all data collected by governments and commercial research firms as well as information contained in company records and data previously gathered by other researchers.

SECONDARY RESEARCH

Research using secondary data (data collected for one purpose and used for another purpose later) that can be found by somebody sitting at a desk. This is usually the first stage in any marketing research project. Find out what is already known about a MARKET before setting out to do FIELD RESEARCH in order to collect primary data.

SEGMENTATION

See MARKET SEGMENTATION

SELECTIVE DISTRIBUTION

A manufacturer's distribution of products to certain specific retailers only. Examples include retailers who guarantee to buy a certain quantity within a certain time and those who agree to give the products prominence in their window displays.

SELF-LIQUIDATING OFFER

A sales PROMOTION most easily explained by means of an example: a manufacturer offers customers who buy Product *A* at its regular price a chance to buy Product *B* at a price well below its normal price, usually at least a third less.

The customer has to send the manufacturer some proof of purchase of Product *A* — a box top, for instance — along with payment for Product *B*. The manufacturer will have acquired Product *B* at low cost, perhaps as a stock-clearance item or a bulk purchase from another manufacturer. So the price paid by customers who take up the offer, though well below the retail price, will still be high enough to cover the cost of Product *B* to the manufacturer. The offer, which promotes the sales of Product *A*, thus pays for itself; it is self-liquidating.

Popular items typically offered by manufacturers in this kind of promotion are T-shirts, mugs, or kitchenware.

SELLER'S MARKET

A situation in which consumers want to buy more of a particular type of goods or services than are being supplied.

Economists say that in such a situation the price of the goods or services will rise, attracting other players into the MARKET. That in turn will increase the supply to such an extent that it might become the exact opposite: a BUYER'S MARKET.

Such logic does not apply in cases like telecommunications, where the initial capital investment required to become a supplier is prohibitively high. It does not apply either when barriers such as import controls prevent competitive products from entering a market.

SHARE OF VOICE

That proportion of all the ADVERTISING for products in a particular market that is accounted for by a single one of them. Also known by its acronym, SOV.

SHELF LIFE

The amount of time that a PRODUCT (particularly foodstuffs) can remain in a salable condition on the shelf of a store. Date-stamping the product indicates when its shelf life ends and its shelf death begins.

The expression has come to have a wider use: an artless young actress can be said to have a short shelf life as a screen siren; this summer's Gianni Versace evening wear has a shelf life of a season (until it can be resurrected in 20 years' time as an "antique").

SHRINKAGE

A euphemism for the stock in a retail outlet that disappears without being recorded in the cash register. Shrinkage is the stock that is damaged, shoplifted, stolen, or (in the case of perishables) left over and thrown away or given away.

SIC

See STANDARD INDUSTRIAL CLASSIFICATION

SIMULATION

The acting out of a real marketing situation for the purposes of testing a product. Two types of simulation are used in MARKETING.

1. Computer simulation. Data are fed into a computer and the outcome of a range of possible actions compared. For example, an advertiser might want to test the effectiveness of various media options. A computer simulation could indicate the probable consumer behavior resulting from various advertising actions (television commercials at a variety of times, newspaper advertisements on different pages on different days, and so on).

2. Laboratory simulation. This is often used to test brand purchasing behavior, particularly with respect to price. In a simulated store a group of shoppers is invited into a room, given a sum of money, and asked to spend it on a presented range of branded products. After completing their purchases the shoppers are suitably diverted while the prices on the products are changed. They are then given another sum of

money to spend, and the differences (if any) in their choices are noted.

SKIMMING

A pricing strategy often used when a **PRODUCT** is introduced into a **MARKET**.

New products tend to be price-inelastic — that is, the demand for them is relatively insensitive to their price. Therefore the price maker intent on skimming sets a high price for the product in the early stages of its life cycle. That attracts a consumer group that values the prestige of owning something new to the market or that equates high price with high quality.

As the product matures and sales slow down, the price is lowered in order to attract new customers into the market. Prices may be reduced several times in this process of skimming.

Skimming is particularly appropriate for marketing things like cameras, pocket calculators, and video recorders.

SLOGAN

A memorable and apposite saying about a **PRODUCT** that helps keep it at the forefront of consumers' minds. The best slogans are sometimes witty and often simple.

SOCIAL GRADING

A system for classifying social status. The system in the socially conscious United Kingdom was developed for the Institute of Practitioners in Advertising and is based on the occupation of the head of household (see table next page).

In the United States there is no standard system of social grading. Many American marketers consider it a less useful tool for segmenting consumers than systems based on other factors such as **LIFESTYLE** or neighborhoods (see **ACORN**).

% of Population	Social Grade	Social Status	Occupation of Head of Household
3	A	Upper middle class	Higher managerial, professional
14	B	Middle class	Intermediate, managerial
22	C1	Lower middle class	Clerical
29	C2	Skilled working class	Skilled manual worker
18	D	Working class	Unskilled manual worker
14	E	Lowest level	State pensioner, widow, casual worker

Source: JICNARS National Readership Survey.

SOCIAL MARKETING

MARKETING applied to ideas, causes, or practices. Typical examples are antismoking campaigns and campaigns to encourage the wearing of seat belts. Both try to change people's habits.

SOFT SELL

The use of quiet and restrained methods of MARKETING a PRODUCT — for example, advertisements that rely on associations (of love, warmth, nostalgia, and such) rather than on the insistent repetition of a brand name or slogan. The opposite of HARD SELL.

Inventors, scientists, engineers, and academics in the normal pursuit of scientific knowledge gave the world in recent times the laser, xerography, instant

*photography, and the transistor. In contrast,
worshippers of the marketing concept have
bestowed upon mankind such products as
new-fangled potato chips, feminine hygiene,
deodorant, and the pet rock.*

R. H. Hayes and W. J. Abernathy, *Harvard Business Review*,
July 1980

SOLUS SITE

Retail outlets that carry the **PRODUCT LINE** of only one company
— gas stations, for example. The term "solus user" refers to
consumers who use only one brand: the person who drinks only
Smirnoff or drives only Jaguars.

SOV

See **SHARE OF VOICE**

SPECIALIST RESEARCH

MARKETING RESEARCH into particular aspects of markets and
MARKETING. A.C. NIELSEN specializes in retail audits; other firms
specialize in agriculture, children, the **MEDIA**, motoring, **PACK-
AGING**, pharmaceuticals, and tourism.

SPONSORSHIP

The subsidizing of an event, usually sporting or artistic, by a
company for advertising purposes. Events receiving wide media
coverage bring the sponsoring company's name and its products
to the attention of millions of viewers and at the same time
associate it with a pleasurable experience.

Sports sponsorship has grown fast in recent years and now
accounts for more than 80% of all sponsorship; arts sponsorship
has also grown and is especially favored by companies not normally associated with culture — banks and oil refiners, for ex-

ample. Texaco sponsored Saturday afternoon broadcasts of the Metropolitan Opera for many years.

For some, sponsorship is a way of getting around advertising restrictions. No longer allowed to advertise on television, cigarette manufacturers are enthusiastic sponsors of sports like motor racing (Marlboro), tennis (Virginia Slims), and cricket (Benson & Hedges).

STANDARD ADVERTISING REGISTER

Two directories are invaluable to the advertising industry in the United States:

- *Standard Directory of Advertising Agencies*
- *Standard Directory of Advertisers*

They are known collectively as the Red Books, after the color of their covers.

STANDARD INDUSTRIAL CLASSIFICATION

A standardized classification of industries and INDUSTRIAL GOODS that is standardized only so far: there is an SIC in the United Kingdom and another in the United States. Although not identical, they are very similar. Both are based on a decimal code, and all government statistics on industrial products in both countries are published under SIC codes.

For example, in the United States a pair of pliers is number SIC 342311. The first two digits identify the basic industry. The numbers 19–39 are allocated to manufactured goods, with the number 34 belonging to fabricated metal products. The rest of the digits are as follows:

- Third: industry group (2 = cutlery, handtools, hardware)
- Fourth: specific industry (3 = hand and edge tools)
- Fifth: PRODUCT CLASS (1 = mechanics' hand service tools)
- Sixth: PRODUCT (1 = pliers)

STANDARDIZATION

There are two meanings.

1. A process of cutting down on the variety of products produced, often to enable a manufacturer to make economies of scale. Some of these economies may be in a company's advertising budget, so advertising agencies have little to gain from standardization.

2. The introduction of generally accepted standards for the manufacture and/or sale of products. This may be for genuine reasons of health (as in food packaging) or safety (as in the marking of drug doses). It may sometimes go beyond this and become standardization for its own sake, a practice that the European Commission seems particularly fond of.

STOCK CONTROL

The management of the inventory in retail and wholesale outlets. Inventory represents capital tied up, and skillful stock control will keep it at levels high enough to ensure that goods are available when customers want them, but not so high that capital is tied up unnecessarily on a warehouse shelf. For a RETAILER, stock control is a major factor in determining profitability.

STORYBOARD

A device that shows the elements of a television commercial. The board is composed of a series of frames carrying — in sketch or cartoon form — the idea of the commercial and its development. Storyboards are an essential tool in the creative departments of advertising agencies, and they are also sometimes used in the pre-testing of advertisements.

In 1850 a Bavarian immigrant to the United States by the name of Levi Strauss made a pair of blue trousers with distinctive metal rivets.

Levi's were born. They were made of a tough cotton cloth that had first been manufactured in the town of Nîmes in France. The cloth from Nîmes (de Nîmes) came to be called denim.

STRATEGIC BUSINESS UNIT

Within a company, an autonomous division responsible for planning the MARKETING of one of the company's major product ranges. Strategic business units (SBUs) have often been created in an attempt to focus more managers' minds on long-range profitability rather than on short-term profits. SBUs are accountable to top management but are independent of one another. They may well serve completely different markets, grow at different rates, and have different competitors and objectives. Product reduction might be the objective of one SBU, while the addition of a new product might be the goal of another.

A good example is General Foods, which has six SBUs:

- Breakfast foods
- Beverages
- Main-meal products
- Coffee
- Desserts
- Pet foods

STRUCTURED INTERVIEW

An interview in which the interviewer asks questions exactly as they appear in the QUESTIONNAIRE, adding nothing and explaining nothing to the respondent. The respondent may answer only "yes," "no," or "don't know."

This impersonal technique produces data that can be tabulated quickly and easily. But it places a heavy burden on the designer of the questionnaire. Inaccurate data resulting from badly constructed questions may slip by undetected.

SUBLIMINAL ADVERTISING

The presentation of an advertising message in such a way that the consumer is unaware that he or she has received the message — for instance, as an image flashed on a cinema screen for less than 10 seconds, too short a time for it to have registered with the eye.

Subliminal advertising was made illegal in the 1950s after regulators had palpitations at the thought of its potentially manipulative power. However, very little is known about the strength of the trace that is left in the brain by such messages.

SUCCESSFUL IDEALIST

A type of consumer identified in recent research into lifestyles that are common across Europe. (See LIFESTYLE)

It is not enough to succeed. Others must fail.

Gore Vidal

SUPERMARKET

A large, high-volume, self-service store. Supermarkets are usually operated on low-margin, high-turnover basis, and now dominate the grocery trade. Supermarkets are making inroads into other product fields as well, including pharmaceuticals and home improvements.

The supermarket — cash-and-carry grocery retailing — was introduced by John Hart Ford when he started the Great Atlantic and Pacific Tea Company (A&P) food stores in 1912. Clarence Saunders opened his Piggly-Wiggly stores in 1916, pioneering self-service and customer checkouts.

A supermarket is distinguished from a SUPERSTORE or HYPERMARKET by its smaller size (less than 25,000 square feet) and its greater concentration on food products.

SUPERSTORE

A large, modern store, technically 25,000–49,000 square feet, located next to a free parking lot large enough to hold at least 250 cars.

Superstores sell foodstuffs predominantly, but up to 30% of their sales area is typically devoted to nonfood items, primarily hardware and auto accessories. There is a fairly fine distinction between hypermarkets, superstores, and supermarkets. It has mostly to do with size: hypermarkets are the biggest, supermarkets the smallest.

SURVIVOR/SUSTAINER

Two categories in a well-known U.S. classification of consumers (see LIFESTYLE).

SWOT ANALYSIS

An mnemonic for four key things to be considered in any planning company's process:

* Strengths
* Weaknesses
* Opportunities
* Threats

Strengths and weaknesses are factors internal to the company. An excellent service network and a widespread distribution system are the sorts of things that might be identified as particular strengths; poor cash flow and an overextended PRODUCT MIX would count as particular weaknesses.

Opportunities and threats are factors external to the company. Careful scanning of the business environment for new technological developments might reveal opportunities. Threats might come from changes in consumer behavior, from government legislation, or from some major international incident.

*You can trust a crystal ball about as far
as you can throw it.*

Faith Popcorn, U.S. futurologist

SYNDICATED RESEARCH

Large-scale marketing research that is undertaken by a marketing research firm of its own accord and is then offered for sale. Syndicated research is not undertaken specifically for a client. A.C. NIELSEN's retail audit is an example.

SYSTEMS SELLING

Selling a total system rather than an individual product. A manufacturer of robots will try to sell a robotic system that suits an entire production line, rather than just one robot for a single operation.

Although buying whole systems costs the purchaser more in the short term, the hope is that a complete and compatible system will operate more efficiently than would components purchased separately.

Tachistoscope

A device for measuring the extent to which a consumer registers the **BRAND** (or other relevant information) displayed on a package. The tachistoscope shows pictures of a package for various time periods, and helps researchers test the effectiveness of its **DESIGN**, **COLOR**, or brand name before the **PRODUCT** is thrown into the cruel, competitive world of the supermarket shelf.

Target audience

The audience to whom a particular **ADVERTISING CAMPAIGN** is directed, defined in demographic terms by sex, age, income, and so on. Only when a target audience has been defined can the process of **MEDIA PLANNING** begin.

Target market

One or more segments of a **MARKET** selected for special attention by a company. As consumers become more affluent and more discerning, it becomes more difficult to market products that satisfy the so-called masses. New products from marketing-oriented companies, therefore, are now usually aimed at specific groups of consumers.

Teaser

A short advertisement that does not reveal the name of the **PRODUCT** being advertised, but merely states that there is more advertising to come. Such advertisements are designed to tease the curiosity of consumers so that they are on the lookout for the full campaign when it arrives.

Teasers are not new. When it launched Camel cigarettes in 1913, The R.J. Reynolds Company used slogans like "The Camels Are Coming." When they came, they became one of the world's best-selling cigarettes.

TELEMARKETING

The use of the telephone as a medium for prospecting for sales (called teleselling), for receiving orders and inquiries, and for handling customer complaints. The telephone provides the immediate contact between company and customer that is so helpful in maintaining a good relationship over a period of time.

Teleselling has been common in industrial marketing for some time and is being increasingly used in consumer marketing.

The advantages of using the telephone for selling are that it reduces the number of wasted sales visits, and helps identify good prospects for face-to-face follow-up. A negative aspect is that some consumers may regard the telephone sales call as an invasion of privacy.

Teflon is an abbreviation of polytetrafluoroethylene. The Polytetrafluoroethylene Don would not have stuck so well as a nickname for John Gotti, the Mafia leader usually known as the Teflon Don.

TELEPHONE RESEARCH

In most developed countries telephone ownership is universal and 99% of households have at least one phone. That has enabled marketing researchers to use the phone to reach their samples of respondents.

Telephoning is more economical than personal interviewing, and most respondents appear to be at least as willing to talk over the phone as they would be in a personal interview.

Telephone interviewing was developed as a research method in industrial marketing research. It has always been easier to contact busy executives by phone in their offices (see also COMPUTER-ASSISTED TELEPHONE INTERVIEWING).

TELEVISION RATING

A measure of the popularity of television programs based on various methods of research. In one system, sophisticated equipment is attached to sets in selected homes to record which channel the set is tuned to. A **DIARY PANEL** is then used to determine how many people are watching the set. Television ratings (TVRs) are calculated by expressing the program's audience as a percentage of all the households that can receive TV.

TVR can also refer to the percentage of a product's **TARGET MARKET** that has one opportunity to see its advertisement during a particular campaign. It is a measure of the intensity of the advertising campaign.

TESTIMONIAL

The use of a well-known independent person to endorse a product. Chefs are often used for food products; Orson Welles became well known in his later years for endorsing Paul Masson wines; Karl Malden is closely associated with the American Express card.

TEST MARKETING

An attempt to test a new product's performance in the marketplace by launching it in a limited area. Unlike product testing, test marketing requires that the full intended national marketing strategy be simulated within the selected area. Full-scale test marketing is expensive and carries no guarantee that a local reaction to the product will be repeated nationally. For these reasons the practice has become less frequent in recent years, but some consumer goods still do first appear under test-marketing conditions.

J. WALTER THOMPSON

A venerable U.S. **ADVERTISING AGENCY** founded by a nineteenth-century naval commodore named J. Walter Thompson. Commodore Thompson's picture remains prominently displayed in every one of the company's offices around the world.

In 1899, the commodore published a little book of his thoughts that became known as the Red Book. Still read by employees today, the thoughts include such nuggets as "The foundation of most fortunes can be directly traced to advertising."

In the 1980s the agency became British after being taken over by the aggressive WPP. It was not a particularly dramatic change because J. Walter Thompson was for many years (and is again today) the biggest and most respected agency in London.

THRESHOLD EFFECT

The point at which **ADVERTISING** begins to be effective. With classified advertising the effect is immediate. With most other forms it takes time (and money) before new advertising is noticed against the background "noise" of other advertisements. All money spent on advertising is wasted until this threshold is reached. Any company not prepared to spend enough to pass the threshold should not spend anything.

Lord Lever (of Unilever) said that he knew his company was wasting half the money that it spent on advertising; the trouble was that he did not know which half.

TIME-SERIES ANALYSIS

A technique used in sales forecasting. Historical sales data are analyzed in an attempt to discover the reasons for fluctuations in sales over time. Any casual relationships thus uncovered can then be used to help forecast future sales.

TNC

See **TRANSNATIONAL CORPORATION**

TRADE DISCOUNT

The means by which members of a DISTRIBUTION CHANNEL (the trade) are paid for their services. Manufacturers offer wholesalers discounts on their list prices, and the wholesalers in turn discount their prices to retailers. Because they are given for functions performed, such discounts are also known as functional discounts.

Trade discounts may also be related to the speed at which goods are expected to sell.

In addition to a trade discount, manufacturers frequently offer wholesalers a quantity discount. It is also normal to offer what is known as a cash discount for prompt payment. A cash discount might be expressed as "3/14 net 28," which means the buyer (WHOLESALER or RETAILER) will be given a 3% discount if payment is made within 14 days and that the bill must be settled within 28 days.

TRADE FAIR

See EXHIBITION

TRADE-IN ALLOWANCE

A price reduction given for a used product when a similar one is purchased new; an indirect form of price cutting. In car retailing, for example, prices advertised by dealers may appear to be uniform. But fierce price competition takes place between them when the trade-in allowance is being negotiated. In the case of durable household goods (stoves, refrigerators, and so on) trade-in allowances are often nominal and are frequently advertised.

TRADEMARK

A legal term covering words, symbols, or marks that have been legally registered by a company. A brand name or corporate logo

must be registered in order for a company to have the propri-
etary right to use it.

TRADING UP

Marketing slang for moving UPMARKET.

TRAFFIC

The department in an **ADVERTISING AGENCY** that controls the
flow of work between one department and another, for example,
that the production of a television commercial is synchronized
with the production of print advertisements and that both can
appear simultaneously in the **MEDIA** as part of a coordinated
campaign.

TRANSNATIONAL CORPORATION

A term created by Christopher Bartlett, a professor at the Harvard Business School, and Sumantra Ghoshal from INSEAD.
The two professors identified three types of a successful international company.

1. Those (like Japan's Matsushita) that concentrate on economic efficiency through a highly centralized operation
2. Those (like Philips and Unilever) that concentrate on re-
   sponsiveness to conditions in their many local markets
3. Those (like Sweden's L.M. Ericsson) that succeed by developing a specific technology and marketing it assiduously
   all over the world

International companies of the future, argued Bartlett and
Ghoshal, would not succeed with the one-dimensional approach
taken by these successes from the past. They would have to be
transnational corporations (TNCs), companies that combine all
three dimensions.

TNCs have implications for **MARKETING** and for management
in general. Of the three traditional types of successful interna-

tional company, only the second really needed first-class management in all its geographic markets. The TNC will need first-class management and marketing everywhere.

TRIAL OFFER

A form of promotion that gives away a small sample of a product in order to persuade consumers to make their first purchase of the product. Often used with cosmetics and foodstuffs.

Tupperware is named after Earl Tupper, an American who in the 1940s saw the possibility of making food containers out of polyethylene.

TVR

See **TELEVISION RATING**

U&A

See USAGE AND ATTITUDE

UNDIFFERENTIATED MARKETING

The marketing of a **PRODUCT** to the widest possible market, appealing to needs that unite consumers rather than divide them. For many years Coca-Cola very successfully marketed only one product in one kind of container. Henry Ford revolutionized automobile production when he mass-produced the Model T for an undifferentiated market: one model for everybody, in any color so long as it was black.

Nowadays undifferentiated marketing has largely given way to the concept and practice of **MARKET SEGMENTATION**. Even Coca-Cola produces a range of Cokes plus Fanta and Sprite and packages them in cans as well as large bottles, small bottles, plastic bottles, and glass bottles. Similarly, there are now cars to suit every taste, although they retain a loyalty to Henry Ford's ideas of mass production by developing differential exteriors on a core of undifferentiated engines.

When the Burroughs computer company bought Sperry, it ran a competition among its employees to find a new name for the combined outfit. When the name "Unisys" was selected, a headline in The Wall Street Journal asked, "If this was the winning name, what could possibly have lost?"

UNIQUE SELLING PROPOSITION

The idea — less popular than it used to be — that a **PRODUCT** should have at least one unique feature that differentiates it from all its competitors and that can be easily communicated to consumers through **ADVERTISING**. But uniqueness is rare, and it is hard to generate a continuous stream of products with unique features. So the unique selling proposition (USP) has given ground to newer ideas such as **POSITIONING** that are less tied to actual product features.

UNIT PRICING

A form of pricing used by retailers to enable shoppers to make price comparisons among products. Large retailers (especially supermarkets) show the price per unit of a product in addition to its total price.

For example, a grocer might carry four brands of instant coffee, each brand available in three different sizes. Unit pricing enables the consumer to see that a 4-oz jar of Brand *A* costs 50 cents an ounce, while an 8-oz jar of the same brand costs 47 cents an ounce. But an 8-oz jar of Brand *B* costs 46 cents an ounce, while a 4-oz jar of Brand *B* costs 52 cents an ounce.

UPMARKET

Sometimes called "upscale" in the United States. A popular term that (like its counterpart **DOWNMARKET**) refers to the structure of a **MARKET** visualized as having a top and a bottom and a way to move up and down. This dimension can apply across different criteria.

	Upmarket	**Downmarket**
Class	Upper	Lower
Price	Expensive	Cheap
Style	Exclusive	Mass
Quality	High	Low
Features	Luxury	Basic

Marketers use the term chiefly with respect to product positioning and repositioning. Going upmarket might involve increasing the QUALITY of the product — manufacturing in Italy, say, rather than in Hong Kong — and limiting its DISTRIBUTION to exclusive specialty shops.

USAGE AND ATTITUDE

A comprehensive study of a MARKET, including quantitative measures of actual consumer behavior, and qualitative measures of consumers' attitudes to different products in the market. Also known by its acronym, U&A.

The name Valium is quite meaningless, as are the names of other famous Roche drugs such as Librium and Mogadon.

VALS

See **VALUES AND LIFESTYLES**

VALUE ANALYSIS

A technique to help a company find ways to reduce its costs without sacrificing its product's market appeal. Marketing managers and production and design engineers, say, get together to discuss ways that costs might be cut. Ideas are ranked according to their cost-saving potential and are analyzed for feasibility. Any proposed change is then checked against consumer perceptions of the product's value.

Value analysis can be applied to new product ideas when they are still at the design stage, as well as to existing products.

VALUES AND LIFESTYLES

A classification of consumer behavior developed by the Stanford Research Institute and commonly abbreviated to **VALS**. (See **LIFESTYLE**)

Velcro was invented by a Swiss gentleman who wondered how sticky burrs became attached to his clothes. Its name is short for VELours-CROché, French for "hooked velvet."

VARIABLE PRICING

The selling of the same PRODUCT or service at different prices depending on the time or location. Variable pricing is not very practical for large manufacturers of INDUSTRIAL GOODS, but it is a practice found often in street markets or among antique sellers. For example, the prices of fruit on a market stall may be higher on Saturday mornings than they are on Thursday afternoons; the price of an antique may be higher for the well-dressed American tourist than it is for a local dealer.

When buyers don't fall for prices, prices must fall for buyers.

Anon

VOICEOVER

The addition of a voice to a filmed advertisement. Voices are important to the overall impression given by an ad: Infiniti has used Michael Douglas's voice to great effect. But most of the famous voices used in English-language advertisements never get to the exotic locations that provide the backdrops for their voices. They rarely travel farther than the recording studios of London and New York.

WARRANTY

A promise given by a manufacturer to a consumer that a **PRODUCT** is of a certain standard and that if it is not the manufacturer will make good any shortcomings. Warranties are important in the **MARKETING** of certain consumer durables and can prove expensive if a manufacturer has to replace large numbers of faulty goods.

By law, manufacturers must produce a clearly written statement about what they promise in their warranties. A warranty must be neither unfair nor deceptive, and it must be clear as to whether it is a full warranty, or limited in some way. For example, it is common to limit the guarantee on a car to the cost of parts for five years and the cost of labor for one year.

WHEEL OF RETAILING

A theory of retailing based on the fact that retailing is constantly changing; on every main street shops are closing and new ones are opening almost every day of the week.

The theory states that most new retailers start as low-status, low-margin, low-price operators, and as they prosper they move **UPMARKET**, leaving opportunities for new entrants. The theory has some explanatory value. Many discount stores that started after World War II in the way described by the theory thereafter progressed upmarket. The Gap began by selling cheap jeans to teenagers; now it has more than 300 stores in the United States and Europe that are style-setters for the young and middle-aged alike. Other retailers are now selling jeans cheap.

WHITE GOODS

Washing machines, dryers, refrigerators, freezers, stoves: durable goods that at one time were always encased in white enamel.

WHOLESALER

An intermediary linking manufacturers and retailers. Full-service wholesalers used to dominate the business in both the United States and Europe, providing warehousing, a sales force, a delivery service, credit, **MARKETING RESEARCH**, and help with reordering. But competitive pressures reduced the importance of these all-in-one intermediaries.

In some cases manufacturers themselves have taken over the wholesaling function, using distribution centers to supply retail outlets. In other cases, new-style wholesalers have successfully limited the services they offer to retailers (as in cash-and-carry wholesaling). In still other cases, full-service wholesalers have moved into retailing, setting up chains of independent retailers that only they supply.

WORD-OF-MOUTH ADVERTISING

It is every marketer's dream to have a **PRODUCT** so satisfactory to those who purchase it that they immediately recommend it to their friends and neighbors, who just as immediately go out and buy it and then tell their friends and neighbors about it. Such word-of-mouth advertising is very powerful. It is demonstrated, for example, by the rapid spread of the game Trivial Pursuit in advance of any media advertising.

WPP

A holding company that owns some famous advertising agencies and was once known as Wire and Plastic Products (see also **J. WALTER THOMPSON** and **OGILVY & MATHER**).

Historically, the letters "X" and "O" have been unusually popular in trade names. Few are as rich in them as Oxo and Xerox, which manage to have one of one and two of the other. Xerox comes from xeros, the Greek word for "dry," and was adopted by the first copying process not to use wet ink.

Y&R

See **YOUNG & RUBICAM**

The American locksmith Linus Yale, who invented the combination lock in 1862, had nothing to do with Elihu Yale, who founded the university of the same name.

YELLOW GOODS

An expression used for consumer goods that are bought infrequently, last for a number of years before needing to be replaced, and are generally expensive. They include the sorts of things that come under the category of both **WHITE GOODS** and **BROWN GOODS**: ovens, refrigerators, televisions, stereos. Yellow is thus what you get when you mix brown and white.

YOUNG & RUBICAM

An **ADVERTISING AGENCY** with a reputation for being "pure Ivy League" and a chairman, Alex Kroll, who once played professional football in New York. Young & Rubicam (Y&R) also owns the top design firm Landor as well as the leading public-relations company Burson-Marsteller.

When most agencies were rushing to the stock market in the 1980s to raise money, Y&R remained a private and very successful company. Despite the growth of powerful European agency groups it became the biggest "pure" advertising agency in Europe.

YUPPY

A sociological classification that came into common parlance in the 1980s and had special significance for the marketers of fast German cars, clarets, liqueurs, Jean-Paul Gaultier, and the Seychelles Islands.

Yuppy is the acronym for Young Urban Professional Person but is often used interchangeably with yumpy, or Young Upwardly Mobile Professional Person. The yuppy is one of a well-educated breed with a high income and a high propensity to seek instant gratification, even if it means borrowing heavily to do so. The 1980s sprouted several other such acronyms: dinkies (households with Double Incomes and No Kids); droppies (Disillusioned, Relatively Ordinary Professionals Preferring Independent Employment Situations); and the puppy (Previously Upwardly mobile Professional Person).

Zap

The practice of using a remote-control device to switch back and forth between one television channel and another. Zapping is a nightmare for advertisers and marketing researchers. First, it enables viewers to switch away effortlessly from advertisements when they are showing; second, it throws into chaos any attempt to measure rigorously which programs an audience is watching and for how long (see **DIARY PANEL**). Seasoned zappers with butterfly minds can (in all honesty) say they are watching more than two programs at once.

Your legacy should be that you made it better than it was when you got it.

Lee Iacocca